To M

What is life
but the living of it
A Way of Awakening
A Dawn

G Rose Gordy
8/18/12

To Marge

What is life
but the living it?

Stairs to the Attic

A Collection of Poems

Rose Gordy

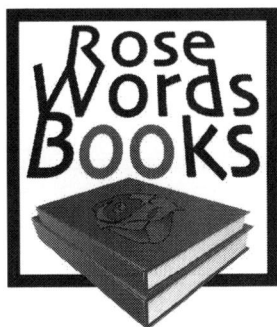

ISBN-13: 978-1466226265
ISBN-10: 1466226269

Cover images and photos courtesy of Stephen Charles and SuperClusterMedia.com

Rosewords Books
www.Rosewords.com

Table of Contents

Part II - A Night Without Dreams Remembered   47

Part III - Laughing at the Oxymorons   93

Part IV - Dancing the Dream of Life 151

Part V - Isle of Lore: Ireland   181

Part VI - And The Flow Continues 201

Dedicated to My Family Here and There

Introduction

This collection of poetry dates back to several poems I wrote when I was fifteen. How they survived is a mystery.

In the spring before I turned eighteen, I decided I had a vocation to enter a convent and become a nun. That summer in a move to start making a break with "the world of the flesh and the devil," I burned all of the writing I had done in the brick fireplace my Father built in our backyard.

Twenty years later after almost thirteen in the convent, I realized I didn't belong in that way of life anymore. Then one auspicious day when I was in my Mother's basement looking for something, I found stashed on a shelf three poems that I'd written at fifteen that had been ripped out of a old notebook. One of these lost poems, "All Alone," (See page 243) is included in this book and has an eerie timelessness about it. Besides the fact that it should have been burned to ashes, it astonishingly captures across all these years what I feel today about the loss of my husband after thirty-five years of marriage.

I have continued to write poetry throughout my unusual life. This includes writing from the early age of seven, through all my years as a nun, through my single days after leaving that hallowed life, through all my years of teaching English, during the era of my nuclear family when I give birth to and helped raise three sons, and finally during recent months with the birth of my first grandchild, precious Elizabeth Hannah. Significantly, my first published poem "To Larry Six Years Later" (See page 116) evolved from an inspiring experience I had running into a former English student of mine in a shopping center.

As I found out first-hand throughout the years, no matter what the situation is, with the will to take that first step and persevere, anyone can change the rest of his or her life.

Rose Gordy
October 2011

The following poems in this book have been published
in the listed publications:

The Dream That Got Away – <u>Dream Network Journal</u> 1995

Big Sur Fantasy – <u>Ginseng</u> April 2011

Slice of Life Flashes of the
             Six Senses of Poetry – <u>Ginseng</u> April 2011

Hour of Light – <u>Burning Light</u> '93

Stairs to the Attic – <u>The Critic</u> Summer 1995

I Dream (?) of Louie – <u>The Merton Seasonal</u> 1991

To Larry Six Years Later – <u>The Maryland English Journal</u> 1986

Speak To Me Tonight – <u>Dream Network Journal</u> 1995

La Nuit – <u>Dream Network Journal</u> 1995

Leaving Home and Letting Go – <u>Mercy Newsletter</u> October 1995

Sky Dreams – <u>Dream Network Journal</u> 1995

Part I

The Never Ending Circle of Awareness

The Dream That Got Away

Was it one whose message
I wasn't ready to face yet?

Or one too good to be true?
Or too strange
or disconcerting
or frightening
to be remembered?

Or was it one that the Angel of my Dreams
kept from my waking self to protect me
to soothe me on a deeper
than conscious recollection level?

Was it one I'll "recall" someday
in a "déjà vu" experience?

Or one that will come back to me
as I live along into it in the future à la Rilke?

So, dear Dream That Got Away,
more power to you!
You're only another dream away.
I sleep for you again tonight.

Published in <u>Dream Network Journal</u> 1995

Big Sur Fantasy

Drinking up the ocean,
I clamored up the cliffs.
Took flight on condor wings.
Became the God of the Sunrise
and the Goddess of the Sunset.

Reveling in awesome,
I sang the sky.
Ate the tides.
Smelled the horizon
and tasted the fog.

But it was not enough.
Flying higher on possibility,
I carved out new precipices.
Tinted the sand turquoise.
Straightened the windy roads
and colored the sky indigo.

Then I flew over the horizon
satiated with my stunning artistry.

Published in <u>Ginseng</u> April 2011

What if the STARS are

ANGELS watching over us

or

PUPPETEERS pulling all our strings

or

SHAPE SHIFTERS from other universes controlling us?

What would we do differently IF WE KNEW FOR SURE?

"Etudes" on the Water

Listening to Chopin
in the San Lucia Mountains of Big Sur   .
at the Hermitage of the Monks of New Camoldoli.

The Pacific, a white blanket
beneath a barely blue sky,
ripples like notes Chopin plays
for me from across the years
to this truly awesome place.

The water flows in various patterns
paralleling the coursing music
I listen to as I watch.
Mellow notes transform into the cottony surface
of the ocean touching the edge of the sky.

Drawn out fluid passionate notes
become the striated lines of the water below.
While the most vibrant sounds translate into a calmness
on the blue green water where waves
are hardly perceptible to my eyes.

Finally, just at the edge of my fine picture,
a different movement stirs on the water:
Compressed waves of sound
reverberate delightfully
in an incessant procession West.

From my retreat trailer I cannot see the shore
or hear the crashing of the liquid notes on the sand.
But I can hear Chopin playing from my laptop
and imagine his music flowing across the Pacific
stretched out so magnificently in front of me.

When Life Begins

Joyous bells peal.
Hands clap.
Voices sing.
Couples dance.

A little one
is to arrive for
her First Coming Out Party!

And so when we come
we also go
because to begin
is to end

because joy
is the flip side of grief

because as soon as
we are born
we are one minute
closer to our death
since all of life
is paradox   contradiction
          oxymoron   anomaly

because we are not meant
to remain on this one earth
we are to be Stars forever
in the universe
of the Spirit

somewhere beyond
life and death
happiness and sorrow
rainbows and storms.

Playhouse 101

It stood in Lois' backyard,
one house down from Barbara's
and one house up from mine.
Built by my dad,
square and wooden,
with two windows,
one on each side
of the one room
with front porch.

We divided the inside
down the middle.
Left side for Lois.
The right for me.
Barbara got the porch.

All preschoolers then,
we decorated our special place
with mismatched curtains
and rickety furniture
from our parents' basements
that fit in the small spaces:
odd chairs from discarded kitchen sets,
a lone small square table,
several handle-less pots and pans
and an assortment of jelly jars.
Especially my little green tea set
Santa brought me
the Christmas I was three.

How many hours
we three enjoyed
playing house there!
Setting our little table
pretending family life.

Wrapping my little sister's hair
in big clothes pins.
Covering it with a lamp shade
to simulate a hair drier.
Dressing up Barbara's
tiny black lapdog Daisy Mae
in a baby outfit
with a ruffled hat
we tied at her chin.
Pushing her around,
our living doll,
in our baby buggy.

Then one sad day
Disbelief!
Horror!
Tragedy!
Lois' older sister and a friend
ransacked our little house.
Ripping down curtains.
Throwing out the furniture.
Destroying all we had created.
Devastating us.

Our house was never the same.
Playing in it was never the same.
We were never the same.
Those mean girls
had forced the three of us
to take the First Test
in The School of Life:

Playhouse 101.

Stuck in a Bermuda Time Warp
2005

Stuck in a time warp here,
hurting from afar
for the residents
of Louisiana
and surrounding states
as Hurricane Katrina
pounds them into submission.

Stuck in a time warp here,
as the price of oil soars
towards $70 a gallon
for the first time
and Katrina knocks
the refineries in the area
out of commission.

Stuck in a time warp here,
as the Sunnis in Iraq reject
the newly proposed constitution
putting the fate of their government
further in doubt.

Stuck in a time warp here,
hearing in horror the tragedy
about the thousand Shiite pilgrims,
mostly women and children,
trampled or drowned
when they panicked
on a bridge in Baghdad
in reaction to rumors
of a suicide bomber in the area.

Stuck in a time warp here
on this island Paradise,
I write stories and poems
and sketch palm trees.
Waiting out the storms
at home and abroad
concerned for
my sisters and brothers
wherever they are.

How Do You Paint?

How do you paint Happiness
that swirls you around in its arms?
How do paint what looks like sparkling stars
swimming on top of the ocean?
How do you paint Love
especially the abiding kind?
How do you paint trees nonchalantly
blowing in the breeze?

How do you paint the joys of Friendship?
Are all the colors of the rainbow enough?
How do you paint the horizon
when it's meshed with the water and sky?
How do you paint the Loves of Your Life
with even the best fine brush you can buy?

I ponder these questions here
in a trailer I rent each year
overlooking the vast Pacific
knowing there are few answers
but always many questions
to challenge my mind and soul.

So with a sigh I wonder more.
When I leave this place this time,
will I still be able to relish
all of this lovely beauty
during winter of snow and ice
at home on the East Coast?

And when it's dark in my soul
and it seems there's no respite,
will I relive these two wondrous weeks
in the San Lucia Mountains of Big Sur
where it's been like Spring in December?

I smile as the sun of high noon
warms the tops of my bare feet as I write
knowing that answers will sometimes remain apart
from all the many questions harassing my heart.

So Be It!

A Blank Page.
What we were at birth.
Open to all possibilities.
To all eventualities.
To all the hopes and dreams,
nightmares and tragedies
humans face at any one time
in their varied histories.

A Blank Page.
A new baby.
Set up with DNA
for indisputable identification.
Already a being apart.
A separate being
no longer umbilical corded
to a mother.
No longer protected
in her womb
for better or worse.

A Blank Page.
Waiting to be written on.
Waiting to be covered
with important or
just mundane messages,
statements, notes, ideas.
A child new to this world.
A blank page of possibilities.

So we all come into this world
of light and darkness
of day and night
of hot and cold
of in and out
of up and down
of friend and foe
of birth and death.

We travel down
a dark passage
into blinding light.
A warm passage
into shivering cold.
And we cry.
Cry for all
we're worth
or will be or become.

We cry because
there is no going back.
There will never be any going back.
We will be slammed
and jerked and swaddled
into the cold and dark world.
Into its harsh light of day.
Into its glaring darkness of night.

And our mothers
will be at once bereft and joyous.
Losing and finding
will plague them
from our arrival on.
The constant coming and going.
The constant hellos and goodbyes.
The constant letting go's and hanging on's.
The constant joy and pain.
Pain and joy.

And when we are laid to rest
in ground or jar
or as part of another,
our genetic base
will disintegrate or be integrated.
Our blank page will be filled
and crossed out
and added to and revised.
We will wander down
another dark passage
far out into the glorious light.

Into the Full circle
that is existence.
Into the Full Circle
this is Life/Death.
Into the Full Circle that
is the Blank Page
of our unique DNA.

So Be It!

A Poem Before 6 am

"I want the one rapture of an inspiration."
Gerard Manley Hopkins

A line comes to me
on the edge of awakening.

An inspiration ferried to me
from the other side of awareness.

A gift from the Muses
to grace my day

with a new dawn
of inner light.

But it's already evaporated
into the crisp air of morning.

I know I only had it
for a fleeting second.

What more can I expect now?
That it has become a part of me.
On the deepest level of myself.
A line for the ongoing poem of my life.

The Never Ending
Circle of Awareness

"We dance round in a circle and suppose
while The Secret sits in the middle and knows."
Robert Frost

I'm flying with wondrous wide wings
through clouds of total unknowing.
For I am The Question.

Yet I can flow freely too
though clear skies of certainty
since I am The Answer as well.

I dance a continuous dance
inside my deepest, truest self.
Round and round I go and go

while The Secret just sits there
waiting for me to find out
exactly what I already know.

TV Debut

on Lifetime's Author's Corner
April 11, 2011
Florida

Nervous for days beforehand,
as I stressfully prepare myself
to answer a myriad of questions
about my book "Unsettled Lives -
A Collection of Short Stories."

But like a cloud disappearing
in the summer sky,
as soon as I walked into the building
housing the TV studios,
I felt only calm peace and assurance.

Though I had been told
what could go wrong
and how hard it might be
I was all the while not the least bit nervous
or even aware of the many cameras.

It was a Lark. A Fun Time. A Joy.

Les Mots

"Sometimes I fling
myself into the arms of words...."
Michael Kruger

Words fly out onto the keys
born from my fingers.
Labor is the incubation of ideas
and when the time is right,
my water breaks.
The tide flows.
My child is born.

A heart specialist I used to know
told me once that it's harder
to write a book than to have a baby.

Words of joy pain excitement frustration.
Words when no words are worth anything.
Words when only words are meaningful.

Creativity

"Breast-feed your imagination."
Jean Louden

let it suck the milk of you
let it be fed from your deepest self
let it bring its mouth of need to you
let it gurgle near your heart place
let it suckle and be suckled
let it be nourished and nourish
let it cry out for sustenance
     and be sustenance

what if monet had been a writer?

shakespeare a sculpturer?
debussy an impressionist painter?
o'neill an opera singer?
hopkins a graphic artist?
grandma moses a biographer?
o'keefe a dancer?
rilke a composer?
picasso a poet?
chopin a choreographer?
porter a playwright?

is art all one?
is the genius the pride of the creation
or the pride of the creation the genius?

is the vision varied and specialized so much
because we can't be all things to all men and women
or even to ourselves in the one lifetime we have?

do artists reincarnate themselves
as different types of artists
in numerous other lifetimes?

what do we really know about expression,
the creative imagination,
the right brain of our psyches?

what are the mysteries of our minds
waiting to be discovered
by our children and their children?

where do still born inspirations go?
do they hover in the air
waiting to find new fertile imaginations?

and what about those unsung, unknown artists
of every type and genre, what happens to their works
when there's no one to appreciate them?

is it like the old question,
what is the sound of a tree falling
if there's no one to hear it in the forest?

how plant and savor and embrace
new art for the twenty-first century?
who will listen and love and learn?

Unexpected Publicity

South Beach, Miami.
A summer evening in 2011.

An elderly man stops by my table
at a sidewalk restaurant,
puts his cell phone to my ear
and makes a strange request,

"Tell my friend
who you are
and what you do."

I agree and say,
"My name is Rose Gordy.
I'm a writer.
Visit my web site Rosewords.com."

Then the man retrieves his phone
and continues his stroll
perhaps looking for others
to talk to his friend?

Later when my son
returns to our table,
he is incredulous
at my surreal story.

A Spring Morning Walk
in Amish Country

The rippling creek to my right meanders along with me
while the chirping birds enjoying the day's first feast
wing along with me too as I reach the crest of the hill
and look out down the long paved road
heading from farm house and field
to farm house and field.

Newly plowed stretches on each side of the road,
their earth upturned and ready for seeds and green.
I smell life waiting to evolve around me,
a slight odor of manure mixing with the dirt.
A truck passes. The man at the wheel waves.
I wave back.

Then like the debris in the canals of Mars
in Bradbury's Martian Chronicles,
I see a plastic coke bottle
in a ditch by the side of the road,
a Styrofoam cup chewed up into pieces by a plow,
and steps later an aluminum orange soda can
in a gully glittering in the morning sun.

Despite these assaults on the fields' beauty,
I sense simply reaching out my arms
to the breeze of the early morning
will lift me up so I can fly
free and flowing above and across
all of this bittersweet rural reality.

Still I know that here walking this lonely country road
I am closer to the land than I usually ever am,
able at any time to reach down and pick up a handful
of this rich earth surrounding me awaiting birth.
Blessed with this chance to be in touch with nature,
I smile while my spirit sings and soars.

Later back at the B&B a little girl guest
sits awed on the steps by eight tiny kittens,
sorry that the film has run out in her camera
and that she can't take at least one
of the small balls of fur back home.
Wanting more than she can have.

I return to my rented room, to the world of technology,
immersing myself physically and emotionally
in the soothing yet stimulating whirlpool waters
available in the bathroom of this 1800's home,
an unexpected welcomed added attraction
at this place of peace and pleasure on Mt. Joy.

Slice of Life Flashes of
the Six Senses of Poetry

"Poetry is the opening and closing of a door,
leaving those who look through
to guess about what was seen during a moment." Sandburg

1. Sights

first glimpse of the awesome cliffs over the Pacific on Big Sur

a fleeting peek into a house as a couple embraces

hints of memories disjointed in disarray:
a look, a glance, a twitch of an eyelid,
an almost imperceptible motion of a hand

2. Touches

the loving caress of my husband's hand on mine

the velvet smoothness of my baby son's skin

the marble coldness of the chapel floor as I stretched out
for the Prostration part of my Final Profession
to become a nun years before I knew I couldn't stay one

3. Sounds

a haunting flute melody from across a mountain top at New
Camoldoli in Lucia, California

a tiny infant's sneeze twice

the reverberation of the huge bell
of Mount Saint Michel in France
rung by a white robed Adonis of a monk

4. Tastes

cool peppermint lipstick

sweet chocolate cough syrup

the scintillating flavor of an expensive wine
suggested by the Maitre d' of a Bermuda restaurant
my sister and I still talk about more than thirty years later

5. Smells

"My Grandma" aroma of Sister Alma's homemade bread

the salt of the ocean spray during an outdoor massage at Esalen
on the Pacific

the arousing "Come be with me" sexual scent
of a cologne worn by a waiter at a local restaurant
almost leading me to give him my telephone number

6. **Intuitions**

the sensation of being on the right track down a dark path

the knowing what I know when I know it

a distinctive gut awareness in November '96
that I had to retire from teaching,
the same feeling I had twenty-seven years earlier
that I had to leave the convent

Published in <u>Ginseng</u> April 2011

The Best Buys at
Two Book Signings

Baltimore, Maryland
at Greetings & Readings Bookstore:

A young mother buys my novel,
"The Ladies Baltimore,"
and "Into The Green Unknown,"
my collection of sci-fi stories and poems
for her adorable ten year old son
to give to his teacher Ms Taylor
as an end of the school year gift.

Swanton, Maryland
at the Fireside Deli and Wine Shop:

A grandmother buys
all three of my books,
and has me sign each one
for a different grandchild,
the youngest only nine.

Still Turning

The world's still turning
round and round it goes
when it stops
nobody really knows.

No matter what uncertainties.
No matter what concerns
No matter what fears real or unfounded,
we're part of a piece of the picture.

A very small piece
of the puzzle of life.
Trying it fit in
with family, friends, strangers.
Trying to make the connections
that will give meaning to our lives.
Trying to become a viable link to others
in the grand scheme of things.

Puzzles parts pieces.
Pieces puzzles parts.
Parts pieces puzzles.

Liquid Hope or Inner Lemonade

Playing a new tape inside me.
A Flowing Tape called:
Wanting nothing.
Accepting whatever.
Glorying in it all.

Knowing that "to those who love God,
all things work together unto good."
Or as the Zen Masters would put it,
"Be emptiness and you will be truly happy."

Refusing to be negative.
Accentuating the positive.
And with explorer Robert E. Peary,
resolving "To find a way or make one."
To which I have always added
"Or be one."

Making my Liquid Hope
into my Inner Lemonade.

Red on Black

The First Cardinal of Spring
seems to stare at me
from the skeleton branch
of a young Dogwood
outside the upstairs window
where I write
this damp and dark afternoon
in early March
then wings away
across the stark forest.
Birds and omens.
Invasions and politicians.

Which bird will I see tomorrow?

All the Good in Spite of the Evil

I learned a major lesson of my life
when I was twenty-two:
there are terrible things in the world,
all the lies, wars and politics,
that such evil exists is no surprise,
but it is the strength of those who
are honest and good which astonish me.

A professor near retirement had put it best
when he said to us one day,
"As I get older, I don't wonder so much
at all the evil in the world,
but of all the good in spite of it
all along the way."

The Afghanistan
Around the Corner

How do we know
when we'll be tested
or where?

It could be abroad
in an unknown country,
but more likely it'll just be at home.

When nothing goes right
and we can't do enough
as our husbands sit glued to the TV box.

When our kids all want our attention,
but our friends aren't there for us
when we need them the most.

Our battles aren't always
on some foreign soil far away
but instead on the one right inside

where we don't recognize ourselves
and what we've become overnight
in an ongoing inner war we fight every day.

So though we wander afar concerned,
the near is the place where we need to stay
living the challenges of every fine day
on our way to an ever Elusive Peace.

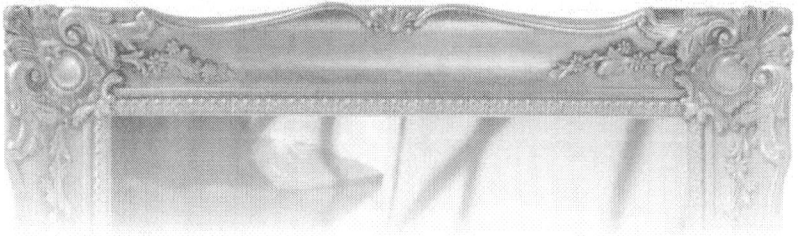

Part II

A Night Without Dreams Remembered

Johnny on the Spot

By any other name
his story would have been
surprising and significant...

Driving up the sacred mountain
where his teenage friend had died,
picking up a tall tree of a man
carrying people-sized bags of food,
lunging them into his trunk,

engaging in a short conversation
about the man's life
under ground as a Lumerian,

watching him disappear,
never finding the entrance
to his nether land.

My Song of the Crow

"You pick out
your own song from the uproar
line by line,
and at last throw back your head and sing it."
from "The Sorrow Dance" by Denise Levertov

First grade music class

The nun lines us up as various birds
by the way we sing.

How well I remember
being the Last in Line.

The Crow.

∽ ∾

Almost fifty years later
in another time and place,

a new friend who hears my story
sends me a quote about crow's significance

from a book by Carson,
<u>Discovery of Power Through the Ways of Animals</u>.

"Crow knows the unknowable mysteries of creation
 and is the keeper of all sacred law....
With crow medicine you speak in a powerful voice
 when addressing issues that for you seem
 to be out of harmony or unjust."

And for once after all these years,
I sing to have been called crow!

Hour of Light

"God of my numbered hairs, I speak as one
redeemed but still at odds with blood and bone."
Sam Hazo "Epitaph en Route"

The Roofless Church
New Harmony, Indiana
September 1, 1969
Noon.

I stood moved, shaken,
Oddly knowing yet oblivious.
A magnificence
A spectaculance
Before me!
If I let myself
Feel whatever is coming,
I'll cry I knew and said.
Then from inside the words,
"I will. I will. I will
let happen the inevitable
whatever it is or becomes."

I walked slowly out
beyond to where sky and field
lay summer beautiful.
I breathed,
I sighed.

Then GLORY.

A tingling,
a sparkling
in my fingertips.
Life came as though
I were completely conscious
of light and surge and
my exit from the womb.

As though finally
Actually born
only thirty years
After.

Life! What Joy!
Resolution! What Relief!
Insight clear and crystal
Happiness only tears could express!

And now...
Now the other side of Light.

Now the pinching, piercing, probing,
gnawing questions,
the whys of the night.

"At odds with blood and bone."
Where is the Light, "Oh God of my numbered hairs,"
And why is the Dark so impenetrable?

Published in <u>Burning Light</u> '93

Telos -
"Communication with spirit"

"from...travesty to...majesty"

"One step from Below
and One step from Above,
in the Divine walk through life,
meeting as One in the Stars."

"For life is a circular ladder,
which, when climbed
in harmony and love,
will bring all on its rungs
to higher sates of evolution."
  Aurelia Louise Jones

After several years
of having the book
without reading it,
I finally do
in one afternoon
on either the recliner
in my office
or on the hammock
on my veranda.

So much of it
resonates with me
though my mind
thinks it has to question acceptance
regarding the ascended Lumerians
past and present.
No matter because
my Heart desires to accept
and live the Truth.

For now we have chosen
to live in this Realm
pretending we are all separate.
Behind the veil,
eyes half open.

But I believe
we truly are not alone
whether inside the earth
like at Mt. Shasta
or in the vast oceans
or far up in the cosmos.

I've always had the sense
we are ALL ONE.
In the Dance of the Universe.
In the "Higher Dimensions of Light."

Dream March

weekend R&R
at the beach

I see flood waters surging through a building
apparently coming from the mountains above.

I speed on foot to warn a group of people
I know are in a place in its path.

I climb mountains and rappel down them
without benefit of ropes!

I swim across a huge water way,
the oldest of my three sons at my side.

Incongruously all the while my sense is
I'm in the basement of the Motherhouse

of the order where I used to be a nun as a young adult
and thought I'd never leave or ever marry.

Let alone have any children because
I didn't consider I had anything good to share.

Then.

The Quicksand of the Obvious

Why is it a person can
see or know clearly
what another should do
in a challenging situation,
but can't see or know clearly
what to do or how to act
in a similar predicament
for himself or herself?

Too close to see?
Too blocked to see?
Too stubborn to see?
Too out of it to see?
Too blind inside to see?
Vision on each side shaded.
Peripheral sight down for the duration.

I'm sure I've been locked
in the same darkness on occasion.
Closed off to the obvious.
Head in the ground ostrich style.
Sunk in the quicksand of the obvious.
Not able to see the bigger picture.
Or even the smaller one for that matter.

It's all a question of perspective.
Of attention. Of acceptance.
To view beyond seeing.
To touch beyond feeling.
To sniff beyond smelling.
To perceive beyond hearing.
To savor beyond tasting.

The Song of My Last Year
in the Convent

"Is that all there is? Let's go on Dancing."
Peggy Lee from her popular song in the late '50's

Dedicated To Crissie, Barbara and Anna Mary,
"The Scarlet Women Of The House," As Barbara dubbed us

One day we didn't say our required psalms
because we were sick in bed.
And nothing happened.

Another day we didn't say them
because we lost track of time and forgot.
And nothing happened.

Then another day we didn't say them
because we were too lazy.
And still nothing happened.

Finally one significant day
we purposely didn't say them
and still nothing happened again!

On none of these occasions
did the earth open up
and suck us into the depths
of fire and brimstone forever.

No devil carrying a silly pitchfork
dragging a long black tail behind him
bounced on our bodies grabbing our souls
to cart them back to Hell with him.

Peggy Lee's song became a metaphor

for the brainwashing we as "good sisters"
had bought into not realizing
that we had been so duped.

It was a form of control as one old nun put it,
to impress on the "fleshy tablets of their hearts,"
that serving God meant giving up everything,
even down to the very things which made us human:
our thinking selves.

A decade down the line
when we finally saw through
the facade of "their" power over us,
we sang with a rollicking lilt in our voices,
"If that's all there is,
definitely let's go on dancing!"

So we did right out the door!

∞ ∞

Thirty years to the night after I made the decision
to leave this life of mind control,
Crissie would tell me she just found out
that the rigid nuns from one of the other orders
did call our Mother General all those years ago
to complain, to report us.
Surprisingly, she told them,
"They're adult women. They know what they're doing."

Wonder of wonders!
That's why we were only reproved
behind our backs never to our faces.
Never called in to the Mount.
Never told to cool it.

Scarlet Women.

The Stairs to the Attic

For years after she left the convent
and married a computer analyst
baptized a Southern Baptist as a teenager,
she would invite her ex-nun friends
to her house for a social dinner.

Invariably, they would laugh about the crazy things
they used to have to get permission to do
when they first entered the community:
wash their hair, press their habits and go to the attic.

And as invariably, her husband or one of the other husbands
would ask, "Why would you want to go to the attic?"
Then the beginning of the story would come out:
it was Pittsburgh and very cold in the winter.

There wasn't room for their big wool shawls and boots
in the small closets in the big dorms
so they had to go up to the attic
to retrieve those items from their huge steamer trunks.

The main problem was that every time they got on the elevator
to go to the attic (they always had to have a companion),
it seemed that an certain old nun was standing there
with her huge protruding stomach and very deep voice.

She always stared straight ahead and scared them.
After all to them as teenagers at the time, Sister M.J.
seemed like a dirty old man disguised in nun's clothes.
They held their breath the whole time it took to go up and down.

At this point a question always interrupted their story's flow.
In the beginning it always came from her left brained husband,
"But why didn't you just go up the stairs?"
As one woman they always responded, "There were no stairs!"

And he would on cue incredulously reply,
"Come on! It was a hundred some year old building.
It HAD to have stairs to the attic!"
"NO!" they would repeat. "There were no stairs!"

This same exchange continued for years.
Then one day an announcement came about the first reunion
of all of the ex nuns of their community
to be held at the Motherhouse and she decided to go.

Though initially she thought it might be a ploy for money,
it wasn't. In fact, they were even told to consider the order
their second home that would always be there for them.
(Years later the nuns did provide a short term safe haven
for one of her crowd after she left her threatening husband.)

When the nun emcee announced that they could revisit
the Novitiate floor of the Motherhouse (without nuns now),
she knew it was her chance
to prove her husband wrong or, in the outside chance, right....

The women in the group, dubbed "In-ey's or Out-ey's,"
not aware of her agenda, thought she was acting strangely
when she checked out every nook and cranny
of the halls where they had lived for six years.

Walking down the last hall past the Mistress of Postulant's office,
she saw the small four bed dorm where she was assigned
the Saturday she entered three weeks after she turned eighteen.
She remembered getting into her white sheeted single bed

in her long white cotton nightgown as the clock of the church
down the street chimed nine and she said to herself

what should have been her first indication she didn't belong there,
"Oh my God, it's 9 o'clock Saturday night and look where I am!"

Across the hall from this dorm was their old vow classroom.
Next to it was a door with a knob which turned as she touched it.
Lo and behold, there were the Stairs to the Attic!
Her husband, of course, had been right.

As a symbolic action, she walked up the stairs
which certainly had always been there,
to give a kind of "hard copy" life to their reality.
And the women standing with her thought she had "lost it."

∽ ∾

When she pondered the significance later of it all,
she realized that the whole experience had been a metaphor
for all they as intelligent young women had willingly given up.
After all, they had never once questioned why they had to use

the elevator to go to the attic or why there were no stairs.
They had never even wondered what was behind that door
she had found so many years later which actually led to the attic.
They had given up their questions, their thinking minds to God.

And the sad fact of the matter was they had sacrificed too much.
They had given up and away their basic selves.
They had denied themselves and accepted the belief
they had to do it to save their souls, to be "good sisters."

And like all the women before them in or out of the convent,
they let themselves become subservient, non-thinking pawns
in the hands of those in power whether they be
de-feminized nuns in habits or macho men in business suits.

She laughed every time she told this story to a new person.
But under that laughter hid a little piece of regret
about those early years so long ago
when she didn't "use her head."

Losing a part of herself in the process
which took her decades to retrieve.

Published in The Critic - Summer 1995

The actual stairs to the attic

Full Moon Over
Mt. St. Francis Lake

My last night on retreat at the Hermitage,
I paddle the house canoe out onto the lake
much later than usual - after sunset.
I let the boat just float in the middle of the water
trying to imagine becoming the full moon reflected there
and entering its circle of completeness.

And then I remember another summer day
twenty-five years before
at another lake and another time....
On that afternoon of July 21, 1969
a group of us nuns and priests,
along with six young theologians from Europe,
all at summer school at Notre Dame University,
watched as Neil Armstrong walked on the same moon
I imagine becoming one with tonight.

All of us were together in friendship first,
simply to enjoy a day at the lake,
but how much more significant was
the event we shared in that crowded room
as we watched and listened in awe:
ONE SMALL STEP FOR MAN...
ONE GIANT LEAP FOR ALL...!

The Prayers of Innocents

November 2002

Over lunch today with the monks
at the New Camoldoli Hermitage,
Father Michael remarked,
"The current situation could be worse
than the Bay of Pigs."
A harrowing thought which reminds me of
a day in the early 60's during my first days
in the convent, we young nuns
were called to Chapel at an odd time
and simply told to pray
about a major world situation.
No mention of what it was.
No question from any of us.
We weren't allowed to read newspapers,
or listen to the radio then.
And certainly watching TV
was out of the question.
We never found out what we were praying about
and whether or not our prayers were answered.
That is until almost thirty years later
when several of us now former nuns
figured out we were praying that the world didn't end
as a result of the Cuban Missile Crisis.
Could it have been that our innocent prayers
all those lifetimes ago made the difference
and kept the world safe from complete destruction?
And can it be tonight as I sit
with the monks and other lay folk
connected in Centering Prayer
that we will help to change the current state
of what seems to be imminent war with Iraq
and all its subsequent repercussions,
especially in the Middle East?
We can all but hope and continue to pray.

Macro Challenge

"Your sense of self is the filter through which you live your life."
Diane Pike

Trying to understand:

the ineptitude
of some

the illogical decisions
of others

the irrational actions
of a few

the inexplicable mysteries
of the universe

and especially
the greatest enigma of all:

My own self.

To Take the First Step

A portal
An entrance
An awareness
Lucidity!

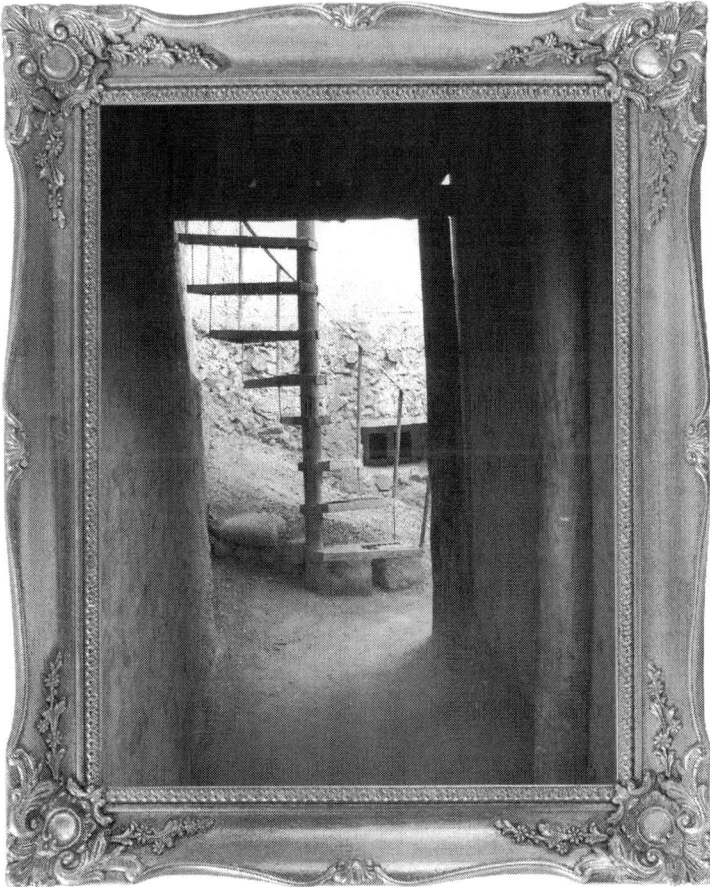

The Catch-22 of Human Existence

FATE.
THE WILL OF GOD.
KARMA.
SYNCHRONICITY.

Are they all the same in the end?
Each a part of the whole
of a Life Lived and Loved and Learned?
        Or
Are they each real or true or believed
depending on each person's upbringing
or indoctrination as an "individual?"
        Or
Are they beyond us, inside us or both?
Immutable forces or ongoing changing ones?
        Or
Are they determinants of our destinies?
Or do we make what is to be all by ourselves?
        Or
Are there parallel universes
like the children's "CHOOSE YOUR ADVENTURE"
where what we "chose" not to do or be happens
and we go off on different tangents
to completely different lives?

Can we truly and actually change our histories?
Or are we bound by forces outside ourselves
to go where we are inexorably led
and become what we would not perhaps
even if we really could choose?

Where IS the line drawn
between free choice and no choice?
Between selection and rejection?
Between choosing and being chosen?

Are we stranded on an infinite loop
into our futures
that we can't get off?

Or can we by conscious human choice
break out of that circle
into another and another and another
by our own free wills?

Are these myriad futures possible for us
on that infinite loop from now
into all our thens?
Or is the Wheel of Fortune
rigged for or against us
by forces we couldn't control
even if we tried?

In the end how free can we ever really be
despite laws, genetics,
psychology and religious beliefs?
Despite the unknown,
the un-understood,
the inexplicable mystery
of what it means to be human:
that on the two sides
of the coin of our existence
to live means also to die
with no control for us
to bypass that FINAL DAY
no matter what we believe.

FATE.
THE WILL OF GOD.
KARMA.
SYNCHRONICITY.

How much do we control
in this puzzle, this conundrum,
this Catch-22 of human existence?

Oxymorons of Life

"Stretch your practiced powers until their tension
spans the distance between two contradictions." Rilke

"For when I am weak
then I am strong.
Power is made perfect
in infirmity." St. Paul

A Budget Luxury Apartment in an ad
A Jumbo Shrimp appetizer on the menu
An Honest Politician on the tube
Friendly Fire across the battlefield

Sadness in people's hearts
Cold echoes of each beat
Living death on their faces

As soon as we begin to live
we begin to die.

Every hello
is a good-bye.

The still point of the dance
surrounds the sound of silences.

Thoughts from the Beach

Ocean City, Maryland on May 29, 1998:
The day after Pakistan tested nuclear weapons following
its adversary neighbor India's similar action weeks before

The seascape is awash with a calm and vibrant beauty
as a lone noisy truck picks up sand near the water
and dumps it on a path to the beach.

Looking out from my eighth floor balcony,
I can see the white awning huts of the art exhibitors
as they set up their canvases for the weekend's show.

Momentarily awestruck by the sparkling water
and the incessant sound of the pounding waves,
I wonder incongruously what effects nuclear bombs

have on the oceans and waterways of our world.
My heart recoils at the thought juxtaposed
into the beauty of this fine morning.

In another piece of yesterday's news closer to home,
a popular, very talented comedian and his wife
are found victims of a murder/suicide.

Perhaps they will have the last laugh somewhere now
beyond the threat of nuclear power's destruction.

The Full Circle of Ourselves

"Dreaming Rotates Us."
John Updike

Round and round they go.
Where they take us
nobody knows.

Being everyone and everything
in our dreams:
actor and director
writer and cameraman
props and costumes,
we fly
we are walked upon
we clothe
we compose
we lead.

"ROTATE" à la Webster:
To revolve or cause to move around
a center or an axis;
to succeed or cause to succeed
in a regular order
L. "roto, rotatum," to turn around
from "rota," a wheel.

How do dreams rotate us?
By turning us around to see things anew?
By changing the angles of our sights?
By twirling us around the center of our selves
both upside down and inside out
in some sort of regular order?

They help us
see from new vantage points
hear from new sets of ears
feel with the skin of alligators
or velvet gowns or a newborn baby's
taste with the buds of plants or flowers
smell with noses or nubs or squares hardly perceptible.

DREAMS.
They send us compensation for pain:
fun waltzing at splendid balls
in magnificent flowing silk gowns
or handsome black serge tuxedos.
Or peace floating in the warm womb of inner space
secure, silent and serene.

DREAMS ROTATE US
to memories long forgotten
to visions fled with the sun
to awarenesses before Awareness
to ourselves as we might have been
if we had listened and seen and heard
as the spirit moved us in the past.

In many ways
memories rotate us.
Insights rotate us.
Love rotates us.
Attitude rotates us.
Challenge rotates us.
Friendship rotates us.
All as our dreams
both waking and sleeping do.

Did I dream of my babies
when they were still
figments of my vivid imagination?

Have I dreamt of my grandbabies
while they are still "in the mind of God?"

Have I planned, foreseen
or changed my future
all because of the rotation
of my dreams?

And will I one fine day
discover that the DREAM
of this Life I live
is only to rotate me
to the ABSOLUTE DREAM
my next life will be?

∾ ∾

DREAMS ROTATE US
to insights we can barely imagine in advance.
To places inside ourselves we would never go otherwise.

The past is the present is the future.
Our mission in this time we've been given
is to embrace the full circle of ourselves.

DREAMS.

In a White Peach

I can smell my childhood in a white peach.
I can see
I can touch
I can hear
I can taste my childhood in a white peach.

I had a hard time waiting...
  to smell its sweet ripeness.
  to see its robust redness on the tree.
  to touch the smoothness of its baby skin.
  to hear the swooosh of my first juicy bite.
  to taste its succulent sweetness.

So sometimes then I even ate one still green
from the tree in our backyard.

Mommy!

While waiting for an X-ray of a problem leg,
I hear a curly haired two year old girl
incessantly calling, "Mommy! Mommy!" and
then knocking on the door of the blood test room.
Her shrill and frantic entreaties
lead her mother to try to calm her
from the other side of the closed door.

"Mommy's right inside," reassurance
from her father falls on her deaf ears.
Finally he takes her into the room
to see for herself that her mommy is OK.
When they all come out together,
"Everybody, bye!" she cries out
to all of us ongoing waiters,
as her mother carries her onto the elevator.

∾ ∾

"Mommy! Mommy!" reverberates to me
across fifty plus years and hundreds of miles
to when I was a toddler and my Mom and Dad left me
at Grandma's big red house with the huge staircase.
Now I know Mom was in the hospital
having my first sister Pat,
but then all I felt was bereft abandonment
in the big, old house with Grandma and Granddad.

Remembering too when my next sister Bee was born
and again I was away from home
this time at my friend Joanne's house down over the hill
where they had stars painted all over the ceiling
in the bedroom where I slept
and lots of little girl kitchen playthings.
But I came down with Measles while I was there

so when I finally got to come home,
I had to slip in the cellar way
and go right upstairs to the room
I shared with my other sister Pat
so I wouldn't give my new baby sister my germs.

∞ ∞

I wonder if my maternal grandmother
who left her home in Hungary at seventeen,
never to go back again,
ever cried herself to sleep
yearning for her mother,
at least in those first months and years
here in this new strange country
filled with strangers speaking a language
she couldn't yet understand or imitate.

"Anyu-Anyu
nagyon hiányzol nekem!"

"Oh, Mommy! Mommy!
I miss you so much!"

I imagine hearing her cry
across a hundred years.

Listening
to Carreras, Domingo and Pavarotti in Concert
Dedicated to Pavarotti (1935-2007)

Something archetypal speaks to me
beyond an understanding of their words
and the language of their sound.

Something archetypal cuts across their words.
The emotion in their music reaches me
in the deepest wells of my being.

Music is the universal language after all.
Understood across barriers of language
since emotion knows no language.

It is an archetypal human gift.
A vehicle and a bridge
that links us all.

The questions, the responses,
the ecstasies, the tragedies -
all sung into understanding.

As T. S. Eliot wrote,
"The still point is the dance."
So is it the beat between the beat.

The universal emotion which cuts
beyond time and space
and meaning and understanding

at a level of archetypal insight.
simply accepted,
understood and lived into.

Even the tenors' accented English
goes beyond my native understanding.
Their singing speaks to me

as though the words as not ones
I've heard and understood
throughout my life.

A unique switch
so what is not is
and what is is not.

A metaphor for much of reality.
The cloaking of truth
which is only understood

beyond the meanings of words.
Beyond even an understanding
of one's own language.

Emotion is a language to itself.
Do words ever do it justice?
Can the words of emotion be translated?

Are there words to express it adequately
when only a sound or a melody like a bird's
can express it truly?

When only a look,
an expression of one's true being
in song can do it?

Is there something about Opera
that defies understanding of the language sung?
Of meaning that swells up and out beyond time and space?

That bridges time and space to no time and no space?
To intuition and insight
at once telepathic and instantaneous?

Carreras: His Power/Animus
merged with the softness
of his anima underneath.

Domingo: His Power/Animus-Anima
fused within his unflagging emotion.
The irony of his first name Placido.

Pavarotti: His Power/Anima
housed in the bulk of his body size
where his animus reigns supreme.

The three span the range of maleness.
Yet beyond the traditional male
to the universal gender of all humanness.

I flow into the ocean of these three men's emotions.
I swim in the incoming tide of their feelings.
I float through the roaring waves of their songs.

I fall asleep and wake up
surrounded, inundated, subsumed
into the flow of the music of their songs.

When these men sing together,
I sense the fullness of humanity.
Anima/animus in total communion.

A mix of might and sensitivity
beyond an understanding
of the language of the words.

Rain Music at an Indiana Lake

From my desk I watch a summer shower start
one drop by one drop by one drop
on the lake beyond the water lilies.

The rain falls hesitatingly at first
like a beginner playing the piano,
her fingers on the keys tentative.

Then with a mighty rush from the opposite shore,
it runs full force toward me
in a flurry of fine power.

Chopin's playing his Heroic Polonaise now
with all its wild emotion and abandon
as the downpour cascades across the water

Minutes later the shower settles into a steady fall
bringing no mists to obliterate the shore beyond
as a massive thunder storm did Sunday night.

Gershwin's up next smooth and cool at the keyboard,
his soothing rhythms accentuated by
the haunting wail of a far off train whistle.

As the rain tapers off to a few fleeting drops,
it becomes a little child practicing scales
as his fingers linger on the keys of the water.

The music of a summer morning shower lakeside.

A Night Without Dreams Remembered

THEY SAY we have them every night
even multiple ones.
THEY SAY we just aren't aware enough
of them all the time.

THEY SAY if we tell our unconscious we want them,
they will come.
THEY SAY if we even just write down an image or an emotion,
it'll be enough to start the remembering.

THEY SAY we can teach ourselves
to know when we are dreaming
to fly and do whatever we please
defying earthly laws and our thinking minds.

THEY SAY we can control our nightmares,
and turn them into pleasant dreams,
the sweet ones we've been wishing for
as long as we can remember.

THEY SAY that if we were denied dreaming
by continually being awakened,
we would become increasingly irritable
and ultimately suffer nervous breakdowns.

THEY SAY writing our dreams down
is only the first step in the process.
We have to honor the insights culled from them
to make them come alive and change us.

THEY SAY our dream worlds are as real as our waking worlds.
That one flows imperceptibly into the other in waves.
That the tides of understanding surge in and out.

THEY SAY tonight we could have the end of a dream
begun years ago or the beginning of a dream
that will be continued some fine night in the next century.

SO THEY SAY.

But they don't have to convince me.

I SAY I'm a different, more aware of myself & the world woman
since I managed to push open the door
to my dream recall many Augusts ago.

I SAY dreams have changed my life on every level
personal, social, spiritual, professional, creative.

I SAY my waking as well as sleeping dreams are my friends,
solacing, encouraging, reassuring, reminding,
and sometimes even jolting me
into taking new adventures,
accepting new challenges joyfully,
and believing in the reality of my worth and wonder.

I SAY if more people could be led to recall,
record, study and honor their dreams,
both waking and sleeping ones,
the world would become a proverbial "Better Place."

I SAY there would be fewer breakdowns
into depression and violence to oneself and others
if dream study were a national as well as international
valued and embraced experience.

I SAY.

Come to me, my dreams!
Teach me tonight and tomorrow
All the days and nights
Of the rest of my time here.

Mere Days to Financial Armageddon

The Debt Crisis as of July 2011

If the U.S. Government
was but a citizen,
would it get away
with the current stalemate?
Teetering on default, hopelessly deep in debt?
No, it would have had to pay the piper years ago
with serious repercussions:

Foreclosure on home.
Assets confiscated.
Credit rating downgraded.
For all intents and purposes
he would have become
a "persona non grata."

But not Mr. U.S. Government.
He can call his own shots.
Change the playing Field.
Simply up the ante willy nilly.
And get away with assisted
financial suicide
with no one to blame!

Pay attention, Mr. U.S.
You've made your bed.
Now you have to lie in it.
"Lie" being the operative word.
Because if this current crisis
is a huge whale of a farce
a manufactured doomsday,
then the Powers-That-Be
have fooled us again!
Perhaps they need to be voted out of office
and sent home
to become spectators, powerless citizens.

A Sonnet to the Good in Evil

Children who hate and cheat and fight and steal
unknowing of an unfortunate fate
increase in numbers each day and even kill
without logic though fueled with hate.

Worker bees who waste and blame and mock and lie
with no intention to change a thing
increase in numbers each day and even spy
for other countries where money is king.

Parents who yell and hit and hurt and smile
with no compunction about things they're doing
increase in numbers each day and with guile
pretend to help the children they ruin.

And yet evil still only counts a bit
Compared to all the good in spite of it.

But Not the Living?
Four Variations on a Revision

#1
The town I remember from childhood
was like a sedate and unassuming
old lady in Western Pennsylvania
when we used to visit relatives there.

Today five decades later it has become
like a wild and uncontrollable teenager
my brother tries to counsel
in an almost inner city school.

During a recent gang war
the leader of one group
pushed his girlfriend in front of him
as a human shield to take the bullet meant for him.

Before her funeral my concerned brother
asked if they'd be further trouble
since members of both gangs
planned to attend.

"No," a seasoned teacher on the sidelines
of the youthful battlefield
reassured him,
"They honor the dead."

#2
His girlfriend
a human shield.
Pushed into service
by him a coward
Gang Leader.
Both gangs
to attend
her Funeral.
Asked if they'll
be Violence,
a veteran teacher
reassures a new counselor,
"No, they honor the Dead."

#3
A human shield:
The Gang Leader's Girl.
Pushing her in front of him,
forestalling his own Death.
Both gangs attend Funeral.
There will be no Trouble.
"They honor the Dead."

#4
Human shield.
Honor the dead.

No Penalty for Early Withdrawal?

What many women have been facing
since time immemorial:
Only a hint of the story.
Not the climax.
Being only the vessel.
Never the wine.
Only the cave.
Never the visitor.

Does it really matter
some never knew the difference?
Does it really matter
they believed it was their wifely duty
just to be an opening
to invite a visitor in
without the joys of welcome
beforehand or along the way?
Or even after?

Does it really matter
many thought this was all there was?
Who faced the penalty
for early withdrawal the most?
The women, of course!
To go about their days
without the night's high.
Denied or just altogether unknown
so not even sought after.

Does it really matter
many women knew no better?
My grandmothers and mother among them.
And how many more before and since?
All of them simply to be a place to enter.
A door to open.

Curtains to pull apart.
Have any women ever realized
how many men like banks too big to fail
have never paid
any penalty for early withdrawal?

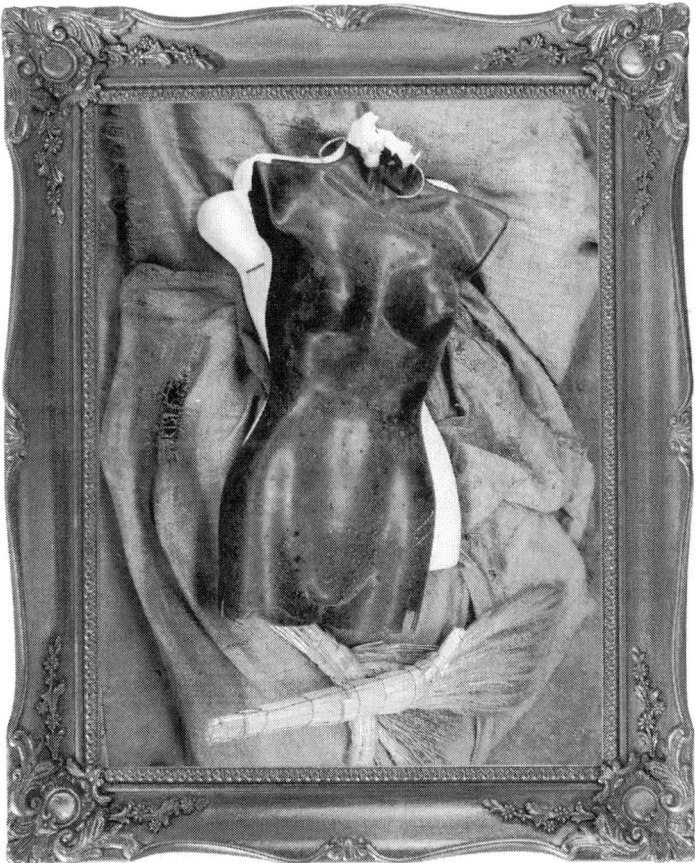

Tropical Man

Trees towering around our house
swaying like anorexic drunken sailors
in the wild wind's path.
Rain cascading form the darkened sky.
Power flickering on off, on off.
Every leaf on my houseplants
out on our two verandas
getting a real workout
right and left, right and left.

Ernesto has come to town
and he's throwing a holy fit.

Give It To The Man!

"All narrative is metaphor."
Mary Oliver

From behind my family at church,
a command from a grandfather
to his granddaughter
when the collection basket was passed,
"Give it to the man."

A metaphor for what women
have repeatedly been told to do
directly and indirectly throughout the ages.

GIVE IT TO THE MAN!
It, a metaphor for herself.
Her body. Her time. Her energy.
Her love. Her attention. Her money.
Her future.
HER VERY LIFE.

Or will they give him back what he sometimes throws at them?
Hassle for hassle? Abuse for abuse? Hate for hate?

GIVE IT TO THE MAN?
But what about this new 21st century generation of women?
Will they continue this giving of their "all" to THE MAN?
Or will they bestow passion and honor and respect on him
with he returning the same in a loving exchange between equals?

More Than Enough

"Whoever remains for long here in this earthly life
will enjoy and endure more than enough."
from Beowulf translated by Seamus Heaney

Enjoying and enduring,
two sides of the coin
of our daily existence
in this vale of laughter and tears.

Enjoying when time passes quickly
without notice.
Enduring when time seems to stop
seconds becoming hours.

Is there ever enough joy?
Isn't there always too much pain to endure?
Is there ever enough fun?
Isn't there always too much to suffer?

More than enough love
and kindness and satisfaction?
More than enough pain
and heartbreak and sorrow?

Yes, all in a life lived long
here in this earthly life.

More than enough.

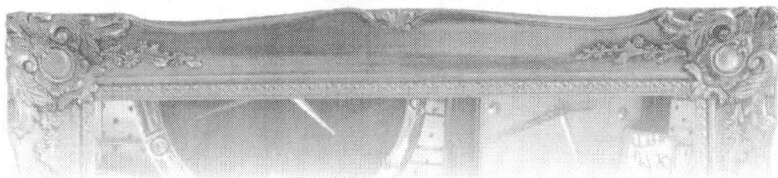

Part III

Laughing at the Oxymorons

Seething into Peace

Anger.
Seething hostility.
Rising blood pressure.

A legacy from my Father
steaming to me across The Long Divide
to this imperfect world where

I have to deal with the discourteous,
the unthinking, the obnoxious,
the un-wellmeaning people.

Injustice.
The "Life Isn't Fair" Syndrome.
Ineptitude.

At times I'd really like to shake someone
into caring about how I feel.
About what I desperately need.

Then calmly settling down.
Breathing deeply.
Cooling off.

Aggravation appeased.
Disgust abated.
Vehemence de-surged.

Seething into Peace
just like my Father usually did
only minutes after his initial upset.

Threats To Peace

Winter 2011

Peace. PEACE. AND THERE IS NO PEACE.
Love. LOVE. YET THERE IS SO MUCH HATE.
Trust. TRUST. BUT THERE IS SO PRECIOUS LITTLE.

We have to realize
in the midst of terrorist attack threats,
disturbing reports form the inspectors
of the nuclear plants in Japan,
political uprisings in Egypt
and war in Libya and Yemen,
that we can't fully seal ourselves off
from biological and chemical agents
or psychological warfare

So What Are We To Do?
Where Are We to Turn?
How Are We to Deal with It All?

Mom keeps reminding me from the Other Side:
"One day at a time and hope for the best."
ONE DAY AT A TIME AND HOPE FOR THE BEST.
onedayatatimeandhopeforthebest.

There is no other way.
Unless it's Sister Regis' advice:
"Live it to the hilt and love it!"

Live it to the hilt
while I have it
and love it all the while.

So that when this life is over
by whatever means in store for me,
I won't say I should have.
I could have.
Why didn't I?

In the end our Fates are fixed.
We can rant and rage
against the Devils of War
in all their forms,
but can we really stop them
or escape them?
The Poor we always have with us.
In our every day midst.

For in the Major Oxymoron of Life,
as soon as we begin to live
we begin to die.
That first second of breath
is one breath closer to our last
which leads us to promise
with F. Scott Fitzgerald
at the end of The Great Gatsby,
"Tomorrow we will run faster,
stretch our arms farther.
So we beat on.
Boats against the current...."

Going on because
there is no viable alternative
unless it's to hide ourselves away
in mind and body.

Relishing life only in a virtual vacuum.
Far from the maddening crowd of threats
but stranded in a world of fantasy and denial.

A Vietnam Love Story

In the mid 60's
they fell in love
in a dusty border town
El Paso, Texas.

She out of the convent a short time,
a newly enlisted nurse in the Army.

He a divorced man with children
who disappeared the day
the two planned to pick up
their marriage license.

Distraught, she got orders to Vietnam
where he unbelievably turned up
skin and bones at her hospital one day
from a stint in the infantry.

Fighting for their love,
marrying in the midst of battle,
a tiny room with no windows
their honeymoon suite.

Love and War.
A True Story.

Reality

Up, down and around we go
on the roller coaster called Life.
Where we get off we don't want to know.
Secrets abound. Answers escape.
We love. We laugh. We dance in flow.

A Sax Tanka

Smooth saxophone sounds
soothe my soul, invigorate
my spirit to calm.
I become the music - cool,
mellow, free, sultry, peaceful.

Dance!

A Found Poem from Rumi,
a mid 13th century Sufi poet

Dance when you're broken open.
Dance if you've torn the bandage off.
Dance in the middle of the fighting.
Dance in your blood.
Dance when you're perfectly free.

Listen to presences inside poems.
Let them take you where they will.

Every object, every being,
is a jar full delight.

But listen to me: for one moment,
quit being sad. Hear blessings
dropping their blossoms.

Be melting snow.
Wash yourself of yourself.

Try and be a sheet of paper with nothing on it.
Be a spot of ground where nothing is growing,
where something might be planted.
A seed, possibly, from the Absolute.

Let the beauty we love be what we do.
There are hundreds of ways to kneel and kiss the ground.

But don't be satisfied with stories,
how things have gone with others.

Unfold your own myth
without complicated explanations,
so everyone will understand the passage
we have opened you.

Let yourself be silently drawn
by the stronger pull of what you really love.

Gamble everything for love,
if you're a true human being.

Half-heartedness doesn't reach
into majesty.

Turn as the earth and moon turn,
circling what they love.
Whatever circles comes from the center.

Dance when you're broken open.
Dance if you've torn the bandage off.
Dance in the middle of the fighting.
Dance in your blood.
Dance when you're perfectly free.

Savoring the Serenity

Sitting on the door mat leaning against the porch wall
of the Hermitage at Mt. St. Francis.

Soaking up the beauty of the lily pads edging the lake
in front of me across my whole line of vision.

Feeling the soft summer afternoon breeze
caress my body refreshing it like a cool mint julep.

Listening to the water frogs
"humfff" "humfff" to each other

and make splashing blobbing "burrupps" in the water
when I least expect them.

The white lily flowers, serene and lovely,
speckle the area of the heart shaped green pads.

I hope to stay here overnight
today, tomorrow or Friday

before I must return to the world
so far from this stunningly peaceful place.

I resolve to take this serenity home with me
and savor it in the Hermitage of My Mind.

Choices and Consequences

A young nun dancing barefoot in the wet grass at midnight.

What did it mean?
Did any of the other nuns see her?
And what if they did?

A young nun standing up for what she believed.

What did it mean?
How dare she?
Some asked, "Why don't you leave?"

A young nun letting two girls use the convent phone at night.

What did it mean?
How could it have been a problem?
Why was it such a big deal to the others?

A young nun realizing she'd been fooling herself for a long time.

What did it mean?
How could she stay now that she understood?
Did she even have a choice?

A young nun leaving the religious life.

What did it mean?
There was only one answer
on the other side of the door.

A young woman being true to herself
that's what it all meant.

Undoubtedly.

I Dream (?) of Louie

"Was it a vision, or a waking dream?
Fled is that music: - Do I wake or sleep?"
John Keats - "Ode to a Nightingale"

We're sitting
on the floor
in the hall
of the enclosure
outside the cells -
a young monk and me.

He asks what
I would do
if I did not teach.
I answer
health field -
lecturer, tour guide.

An older monk -
the Abbot?
sticks his head
out his door.

"Go to bed,"
he tells us.

I wake?
I sleep?
I dream?

I walk outside
on way to 3:30 am
vigils with the monks.

Stars out in full bloom
over the Blue Ridge Mountains
of Holy Cross Abbey,
a glorious full moon
above a blanket of haze.

* "Louie" comes from Thomas Merton's
  religious name of Father Louis

Published in <u>The Merton Seasonal</u> 1991

Smooth Sailing: A Waking Nightmare Turned Dream

Torrential rain.
My green sedan hydroplanes.
Is swept across the left lane
in slow motion.
out of my control
like a horizontal stream
into the guard fence
where it crashes to a stop,
the only sound glass shattering
on the windshield and my side window.

Angels hover around me
as I pray, "Jesus! Jesus! Jesus!"
in my sail across the highway
into the fence
at peace without panic.
Just a realization of the new significance
of the chorus of a song from Church:
"Do not be afraid,
I go before you always.
Come follow me
and I will give you rest"
as I sit in my soft cocoon.
Unhurt.

Surprisingly, a fire truck pulls up beside me
within moments of the impact.
A man puts his hands
around my neck stabilizing it.

Because the fence blocks my door,
fortunately I'm able to scoot around
to stretch out on the board
to be transported to the ambulance
which arrives only minutes later.

My vital signs are normal.
I don't feel any pain.
Only small shards of glass cover me
including one hiding out
in the porch of my right ear
and one in my left foot

which leaves the only blood
on the side of my white shoes.
When I look in the mirror
later at the local hospital,
I lift out a very small piece
from the left side of my nose as well.

In the Emergency Room
I'm checked out as fine,
given a pair of green paper pants
and a top like the ones doctors
wear in the operating room
since my own pants and shirt are soaked.

Many hours later when my husband
arrives from work to take me home,
my totaled vehicle towed to a locked facility,
we drive past the area where it crashed
and I note an indentation in the fence
and a short pole beside it on the ground.
Then I look to the left of our lane
where I see a car pass us bearing the license plate,
"My Angels!"

Ed and I say an Our Father
in thanksgiving for my life.

The next morning I am startled
when I take the shirt I had been wearing
during the accident out of the dryer
and read the words I'd forgotten
were inscribed on it
like an imperative from Above,
"Feel the rhythm of the earth.
Dance the Song of Life."
And I did.
I had.
I will.

Questions on a Sunny Afternoon by a Lake

Why is it we always want something we can't have?
Or someone we can't have?

Why aren't we ever satisfied at least not for long?
Or even not at all?

Why do we go around in circles making the same mistakes?
Not even realizing until it's too late?

Why do we travel up and down the corridors of ourselves
searching, searching for what we think we want
but when we believe we have found it,
it turns out not to be what we really wanted anyway?

Why do all our big plans to be more patient,
more understanding, more loving, more caring
go up in smoke as soon as someone
treats us less than kind
hurts us in our most sensitive spots
criticizes our best intentions
ignores our honest wholehearted work?

Why do we sometimes give in and up too easily
when hanging on through just one more aggravation
might mean the difference between reaching out
and really touching someone or not?

Why am I hiding behind all these we's
when I'm the one plagued by these questions?
When I'm the one with all these problems?

When I'm the one who wants Heaven now.

The Corridors of Myself

I wander up and down
  the corridors of myself,

Anxious and angry and annoyed
  at myself in others.

The Self I cannot,
  will not accept.

The Self that lies and cheats and
  procrastinates.

The Self that argues and denounces
  and threatens.

The Self that hates and covets
  and destroys.

The Self that is the me I hate
  in them.

The Self that is the me I complain about
  to them.

The Self that rants and rages and
  wants to change.

The Me dissatisfied with me.

The Me who needs acceptance from me
  first and most of all.

A Waking Mini Nightmare
in which I meet my Shadow

"It is worth pure gold to know what you are really up to,
underneath your professed ideals."
Robert Johnson from Inner Work p. 73

It's the night after the Gateway Voyage workshop.
I'm sitting next to my British friend Harold
at a gourmet dinner prepared by the host
of the B&B where we're staying.

Across the table at a right angle from me
sits a woman who's name I've forgotten
(purposely or otherwise)
who has come with a couple, apparently her friends.

She asks me about the institute program
I just attended and to share some key ideas about it.
Then somehow the fact of my convent days
comes up and I start to talk about them.

But since she is so her own and only person,
an extremely assertive divorced single woman,
very fashionably and meticulously dressed,
after a few minutes she actually yells at me.

"I didn't come here to be sad
and hear your whole life's story!"
Not thinking I was doing that at all.
I back off, almost completely. Insulted.

But I can't help but hear out of the corner of my ear
snatches of her conversation with her friends
all about her life and hassles and architect career
and a younger man she's currently interested in
but not sure she should continue seeing.

So she's doing exactly what she criticized me for.
Controlling the conversation. Being the center of attention.
Holding fort on her own life and its dramas.

At some point several courses of the dinner later,
I happen to gesture with my right arm
and inadvertently (or not) knock my glass of water over
in an angle across the table getting some on her plate.
She was, shall I say, less than pleased.

If the Shadow is truly 90% gold,
this was a potentially great learning experience.
Though I certainly didn't see it that way then.
But I do have to admit to seeing myself in this woman.

I like to be the center of attention.
I like people to listen to me.
I like people to honor what I have to say.
But I listen too.

Actually I've been told I'm a good listener.
An involved listener. An engaged listener.
I know when to be quiet and when to talk.
I know when there's nothing more to say.
And when to walk away without saying anything else.

Which is what I did that night
after the last course was finally served.
I escaped to my room relieved
to be away from the incarnation of my Shadow.

One Thin Line

Sometimes I feel like
the one thin line of a cobweb
I saw blowing in the morning wind
caught across the edge of the stairs
on the front of the wooden porch
of my rented trailer
on the California coast.

Holding my own
though firmly pulled
in all directions.
Standing my ground
though greatly shaken
to do otherwise.

Safeguarding my own one thin line.

Old Friends

Two dried up
tree limbs
refusing
to let go
of a trunk
hanging on
for dear life.
A metaphor
for long-time friends
growing old together.

White Peaches in the South of France

For Earl, Joellen and George

"A fruit is a vegetable with looks and money. Plus, if you let fruit rot, it turns to wine, something brussel sprouts never do." P.J. O'Rourke

What can I say to describe a bit of Heaven?
White peaches. Luscious to the last bite.

White peaches' season short. But oh so sweet!
Like a reunion trip avec mes trois amis de Notre Dame.

White peaches so quickly eaten. Only stones left.
Like the seeds of memory we each take home.

White peaches. Such simple joys!
Like drinking wine and eating cheese together.

Climbing atop a mountain overlooking the Mediterranean.
Relishing a gourmet lunch at Gourdon.

Surviving the challenging roads of the area.
Delighting in museums of Renoir and Picasso.

Posing for special photos with old friends.
Sharing our hearts' stories into the wee hours.

Later in life…
White Peaches in Santa Fe.
Adobes orange brown.
Sky deep turquoise.
Peaches reddish white.

Friendship:
All the colors of the rainbow.

To Larry Six Years Later

Walking down a shopping center sidewalk,
out of the morning blue
she hears her name called
in tones deeply masculine.

She turns and sees the voice
standing in front of her -
a boy now grown to man -
a handsome man smiling at her.

"Larry?" she exclaims, forgetting his last name,
but surprised and pleased
he has seen and remembered her
and called her by name.

Both adults now,
no longer English teacher and high school junior.

No longer one who cajoles
and one who rejects.

No longer one who tries to motivate
and one who refuses encouragement.

Now just woman and man
who used to work together.

He tells her his current life story -
the part-time deck building business he owns,
the pre-law night school class he attends,
the fire company volunteer work he continues.

She smiles impressed as she listens immensely pleased
that at least one former troublesome student has "gone good."

The she hears him ask, in a more serious,
almost self-conscious voice,
"Do you remember how much I used to hate English?"
She laughs remembering him at seventeen all too well.

The smart-mouthed kid who refused to do any homework
whose only interest was being a fire department volunteer.

The lanky, flannel-shirted seat-warmer who never
even brought his books to class.

The turned-off student who put his head down on his desk
at every opportunity and hated writing most of all.

Her memory flashes recede as he continues,
"But you know what?
I'd like to go back and do it all over
get what I missed."

She shakes her head in understanding.
Maturity comes late to some.
But at least or last
it does come.

Weeks later as she drives home
west on a major road,
she passes the local rescue squad ambulance
traveling east with him the wheel.

And for the first time in her forty-seven years
she wants to be an ambulance chaser
if only to say, "Hi, Larry!"
And celebrate the man he has become.

Published in The Maryland English Journal 1986

New Harmony Anew!

"At times it returns
in the motionless calm of the day, that memory
of living immersed, absorbed
in the stunned light."
Cesare Pavese

It's almost high noon
thirty-five years after
my ecstasy of Birth
at New Harmony, Indiana
when I was thirty.

Flying through the clouds.
Being sun and sky
and All the Glory of the Day.
Crying with great joy
and watering the barren lands
of my inner self.

New Harmony?
Can I relive it today
so many years later?

New Harmony.
Do I still have its feelings
and its insights in my heart?

Where would I be today
if I had never grasped
that one ring of Birth and Light
on the Carousel of Life?

Would I have believed in myself enough
to leave the convent at thirty,
marry five years later
and have three children in two years?

New Harmony
Returning to me now
"in the motionless" calm
of this new day.

New Harmony:
Threshold and Turning Point
and, most of all, Ongoing Birth.

Canoe

For One Week in Summer
as I paddle my canoe.

I am an Indian
on the waters of my tribe.

I am a Settler
in the "Go West, Young Man!" Days.

I am a young child
fishing for my family's lunch.

I am an old man
on my way to streams of gold.

I am a midwife
traveling to the other side of the lake
to assist at a friend's first delivery.

I am a minister bringing the word
to the non believers across the lake.

I am an escaped criminal
who stole this boat for my freedom ride.

I am a runaway slave
hurrying away under the cover of stars.

I am an almost man
on my way to see my best girl
who lives five miles inland
from the far shore.

I am a doctor bringing desperately needed medicine
to the children who live on the west side of the lake.

I am each and every one of these people.
But more of course.
I am myself as well:

An immigrant for a week here on this lake
away from the fast paced modern world
of hassle and competition of treachery and violence
in a money grubbing and status grabbing society.

Laughing at the Oxymorons

"A confrontation with the absurdity of existence
is the only way to remain sane."
Albert Camus

Keeping a sense of humor
about the inherent schizophrenic contradictions
of life's absurdities, big and small:

The stupidity of the "intelligentsia"
who have no common sense to come in
out of the rain of their poor judgment calls

The closed-mindedness of the "teachers"
who do not allow honest disagreement and
even refuse to admit they make any mistakes

The lack of restraint of the "controllers"
who undeniably break the laws of the land
trying to "protect" our "freedoms" and "rights."

The unknowing violence of "loving parents"
who to help their children "grow up"
put them down over and over again

The hypocrisy of the "religious"
who with their inquisitions of every day
belie understanding and love for those they serve.

All of these people rejecting the reality
that they share the same shortcomings
they so ruthlessly condemn in others.

Though hopefully only a few in each group
act in such absurdly contradictory ways,
the stereotypes they create can't help
but enhance the cynicism of the young
who in increasing numbers refuse to become
teachers, police, politicians,
social workers, nurses,
men and women of the cloth
and especially parents.

Oh, the oxymorons of life!
Can I really laugh at them?

Yes, if I want to remain lucid.

The Fourth Time

The driver promised in advance
that Raging Thunder always flew
every day of the year.
But Mother Nature had other plans
She laid her thick cloak of fog down
and didn't let Mr. Sun take it off
in time for our Hot Air Balloon flight
over Cairns, Australia that morning.

∞ ∞

Mountains and Mist
above and below
dark and white.
White chalk
canceling out mountains
to fly through clouds on a plane
different from
on a hot air balloon
clouds like a child's "blankey"
or an old lady's long shawl
or whipped cream atop chocolate cake

∞ ∞

The Third Time
apparently
was not the charm
as the saying goes
foggy weather cancelled
our three attempted
hot air balloon rides

First in Sedona, AZ
then in Christchurch, NZ
third in Cairns, AU

But tomorrow's another day
One more chance
another attempt
with the Hope that flies eternal.

∞ ∞

The Charm.

The Fourth Time.
We got a double trip today
since our trip was canceled yesterday
and we re-upped.

New appreciation
of the awesome sun
rising over mountain ranges
on the biggest balloon in world
with twenty persons but no weight taken.

Our "pilot" Neil
who used to fly helicopters
soared over his home this morning
his farms of mango and pineapple
banana, coffee
with kangaroos and wallaby.

Climbing into the basket a challenge
but my bad leg cooperated.
Our first landing very easy.
The second a half hour later
touched down in a field on its side
with our backs on the ground

much easier to crawl out
as I had imagined before it happened.
Tantalizing red champagne
with breakfast afterwards.

The Fourth Time
truly was the charm.

Early Euphemisms

Growing up in the 40's and the 50's,
I never heard anyone say
someone was "pregnant."
Only in "the family way."
Or "in trouble."
Words spoken undercover.
Behind cupped hands.
Whispered into telephone receivers.
Hushed comments over backyard fences.
In our kitchen or living room
mumbled in broken Hungarian by my parents
so we kids could not understand.

I never heard the word "prostitute" either then.
In high school not understanding
guys' snickered jokes about "Brick Alley."
Only vaguely understanding
it was not a place to go
because "nice" things did not happen there.
One day finally realizing girls and women do get pregnant
without benefit of a piece of paper
and that some even give their bodies to paying customers.
Words like "tricks" and "pimps," "hookers" and "whores"
relatively recent additions to my vocabulary bank.

Also never hearing someone say "homosexual."
"Fairy" or "queer" were the muffled terms then.
Again not really understanding
their full meaning for a number of years.
In eighth grade not comprehending
why the young parish priest was sent away
because he liked boys.

Somewhat better prepared to accept "gays"
thirty years later over lunch

at a filmstrip evaluation workshop.
Talking about the Future Shock movie
I always showed my science fiction students
and mentioning their most remembered scene,
the one they always laughed about,
the marriage of Tom and Don,
when the quite handsome man beside me
calmly announced, "Well, I'm gay and here's my partner,"
indicating the other man at the table with us.

In the early 60's in the convent,
our ahead-of-her-time superior
gave me and another Junior Professed permission
in our first teaching assignment
to visit the PTA president who had just had a baby.
But our principal, a much less liberated nun,
raged when she heard about it,
saying we didn't have a job in her school
if we dared go so, of course, we didn't.
Years later realizing the inherent oxymoron of it all:
not being able to honor a woman who had given birth
to a child who one day would be ours to teach.
Did our first principal think that visiting a maternity ward
would make us hanker after motherhood
and lead us out of the convent?
The irony is though we never went to the hospital,
the other young nun and I did leave the convent six years later,
marry and ultimately give birth to our own children.

Learning many additional facts of life in the convent
from the novels I read for my English major classes
and being cut down because of the supposed salaciousness
of their plot lines when I shared them over dinner
with my fellow college student sisters.

Why was it such a deal in the past
"to tell it like it was?"
Why did women like my mother not even know
what would happen on their wedding nights?
What was the big secret worth?
Agony and mistrust and denial?
Embarrassed long suffering in silence?

If more information had been forthcoming in the past,
how much sooner women might have been liberated,
at least from their own fears and ignorance?
Was it men who did this to them
or simply the well meaning older women over the years
who hadn't been told anything themselves in advance
and therefore had nothing to pass on to their daughters
except their own negative memories?

Does now knowing more change things in the end?
Are fewer girls today shamed and disillusioned
and raped without their understanding as a result?
Or are they only much younger than years ago
so they still don't understand what's happening to them?

Will "dumb blonde" continue to be an euphemism
for women out of touch with themselves and the realities
of lust and love and sex, marriage and commitment?

Will the young women of the twenty-first century
and all the ones to follow them
appreciate what it took for their mothers and grandmothers
and great grandmothers and all their matrilineal ancestors
to survive in the dark and learn its secrets there
for themselves without benefit of facts and support in advance?

Will these new women change things for their daughters
so that finally the circle of ignorance and embarrassment
will end once and for all?

Of Turkeys,
Temptation
and Tenacity

loser dates without futures
still passion surges
need firmness to say no
to him too full of himself though with some reason
or to him surly and sassy yet very pleasant to the eye
or to him muscular & mighty but with too little power or passion
or to him a football player type who can't run the ball or get it up.

women can be tempted by these turkeys
but can be tenacious and say no, goodbye,
be gone, I'm out of here, go home, get lost,
go play in traffic, check yourself out in the mirror again,
get thee gone, you fools!

is there some reason just because a man
is handsome, muscular, funny, outgoing
or any of the above and even more
that a woman has to fall down
and give it up for him?
well, yes, sometimes the temptation
is too great and she leaves her reason
at the door with her purse.
"discretion to the winds," she says,

i'll make hay while the sun shines
so what if he won't be around tomorrow
or if he's just another turkey
i'll roast him good!

tenacity now or later
what does it matter?
i will win anyway.
i'll be in control
when he's beyond control
before and afterwards.
i have it all figured out.
these turkeys won't get me.

just who am I fooling?

High Tides

The waves bombarded the shore.
    Relentlessly.
  Like a little girl asking,
   "Why? Why? Why?"

Seleria sat at the water's edge.
    Distraught.
Like a young mother suffering
   post partum depression.

The sand steamed the heat
of the summer afternoon.
    Mercilessly.
 Like the anger of her father
when he found out what she did.

Seleria stared out to the distant horizon
   tormented by a deep inner pain.
 Like a high tide that kept pounding
    the edge of the beach
     without respite.

Then from somewhere out in the far blue,
   she heard the ocean call to her.
     Softly.

   "Come to me, Dear Sad One,
I will give you surcease from your pain.
 I will give you forgetfulness."

  At that Seleria felt a push and a pull
to stand up and walk into the surging water.
   "Who will care if I disappear? "
    she murmured to herself
    as though in a trance.

She walked and floated and then swam
   far out into the arms of the water
    letting its waves envelop her
    to wash away her heartache.

Finally, she allowed her body
     to float free
with no concern for her safety.
  With no care for anyone.
Especially her own self.

From behind her swimming at an even clip,
    Sebastiani kept tabs
    on the young woman.
   His intuition on high alert
from the moment he saw her walk
    into the raging water.
  Feeling great concern for her.
   For her very survival.

When he saw her body become motionless
    on top of the water,
  he swam faster and faster to her,
   put his arm around her neck
    and slowly but certainly
     with exquisite care
swam her to shore with him.

  Placing her lovingly onto a blanket
he had stretched out earlier on the sand,
   he checked her pulse.
It was weak but she was still breathing!

She didn't seem to have swallowed any salt water.
  He had watched her so assiduously,
    he would have known
   if she had ever gone under.

Now she was safe.
Safe with him who caused her so much pain.
    Safe with him because of whom
    she had nearly given her life.
Safe with him whom her father rejected.
    Whom he could never forgive.

    He honored the pains
throbbing through his soul now.
    Like staccato notes
pounding down on the waves,
they assaulted him ruthlessly.
    Why hadn't she told him?
        Why did "it"
have to end the way she had chosen?

When Seleria opened her eyes
        many minutes later,
    at first they smiled love to him,
but then they turned blank with pain.

    Why had Sebastiani
pulled her out of the water?
    Why had he returned her
to the world of her gnawing regrets?
Why was he still there beside her?
    He had to hate her, didn't he?

    The waves continued
to run back and forth in and out of the shore.
    Like athletes on an endless treadmill.
        Or like two lovers
        caught in an infinite loop
        of love and mistakes.

A Drifter. A Wanderer. A Loner. On Big Sur.

Fending for himself.
Living off the land
and the rubbish of the inns.

With no place to rest his head.
Wearing his only clothes on his back.
Alone on the road.
Or lost in the deep woods.

Drifting with the breeze.
Talking to the birds.
Racing with the foxes.
Sitting on the rocky shore.

A Lonely man on the run at Big Sur.

Three Women on a Raft

To honor Sylvia Plath, Anne Sexton and Margaret Atwood
I studied during an independent research grant

Sylvia, Anne and Margaret,
of the three of you,
Anne, I feel closest to you.

Your images.
Your pain.
The normal.
The mundane.

Anne, Anne,
I know you.
Anne, Anne,
I feel you.

But why did you have to do
what you did?
Suicide - your Hegira,
your flight from danger.

Leaving me
all these years later
to ponder it
to wonder about it
to empathize with your pain.

Oh Anne, Anne,
I hurt with you
even now in your peace.

∞ ∾

Three women in search of themselves.
Three on a raft sinking, sinking, sinking.
Poets, feelers, sufferers.

Gluttons for punishment.
Theirs and what only truly belonged
to their creations
to their poetry
to the others in their lives.

Gluttons for pain.
What truly inspired them
or grew and destroyed them
but for Margaret sustained her.

Gluttons for fame.
Gluttons for fathers.
Gluttons for success.
Gluttons for mothers.
Gluttons for being.

Gluttons for surfacing.
For riding high on Ariel.
For sinking low on Kayo.
For hanging on with Graeme.

Gluttons for work
for images
for loneliness
for waiting
for suffering
and loving.

Three women in search of themselves.
Separate but in community.
Several but one in spirit.

Writing out of personal agony
to the defeat or the glory
of all of us,
whichever comes first
or last
or foremost.

Three women on a raft.
The boat of life.
Two will "drown"
throwing themselves
into the gassy waters of death.

The third will survive
paddling her own canoe alone.
A Handmaid surfacing.
always surfacing.
A Lady Oracle
in a Life Before Man.

So two will go down
coming up with the critics
as they do.

And one will go on
writing it out all the while.

∽ ℘

What is this thing
called life
called love
called survival
called choice?

Called living it to the hilt and liking it?
Called if it isn't worth doing well,
it isn't worth doing?

What is this thing
called poetry?
Is it emotions personified
into hands that speak
feet that cry
ears that smell
hearts that break
like china tea cups
smashed against the wall?

Is it images of death bells
and cuddly kittens
and old ladies in cancer wards
and frogs as princes
and women in red satin dresses
and little girls crying
demythologizing their daddies
or cutting their husbands down to the quick
de-balled and demoralized?

∽ ⌒

Oh dear ones,
Sylvia, Anne and Margaret,
what say you three to me
trying to bud into poet
who knows the frustration

of wanting it all and then some
of hanging out on my limb
and waiting out the coming
PASSIONATELY
just as each of you did?

Somehow I feel
or better know,
I'm out on that raft with you.

I know two of you
have chosen to go under
but only in body.

I know your true spirits
live and breathe
with mine and Margaret's
even today.

Floating, floating, floating....

The Yin and the Yang of Feeling and Knowing

How many times have I suffered the pain
that comes when the two are separated?

How many times have I tried to reconcile
the two in myself to no avail?

How many times have I had to learn and relearn,
sometimes in the very hardest ways,
that there's a problem if the two aren't joined?

Neither feeling apart from knowing
nor knowing apart from feeling
can bring true realization.

Maybe this is the reason
though I "knew" on some elusive level
the year before my Final Profession in 1962

that I really didn't belong in the convent,
that I really didn't know what I was doing
when I entered three weeks after my eighteenth birthday,

it took me almost seven more years
for my feeling to catch up with my knowing
so that I could fly back to my other life.

Georgia's Purple Petunia Print

At O'Keefe's museum
in Santa Fe, New Mexico,
the only one in the country
dedicated to one woman's paintings,
I bought one of her small
purple petunia prints
on a visit several years ago.
Afterwards I stopped down the street
to photograph the distinctive top edge
of the Museum of Modern Art building
across the street from the local bank,
resting my purse and two azure blue bags,
one containing Georgia's purple petunia print,
the other calendars, an appointment book,
assorted O'Keefe pamphlets,
and a number of small plastic pouches
of hand lotion samples,
fig and cassis and mandarin,
from Georgia's museum bookstore,
behind me against the stone wall.

Minutes later
walking up the steps
of St. Francis Cathedral
on the edge
of the commercial area of town
where I was to meet my friend,
I realized I didn't have
my purple petunia print.
For about half a minute,
I considered retracing my steps
in hopes of retrieving it
possibly still resting
in its azure blue bag
against the bank wall.

Then I purposely decided not to.
Instead, I would let it stay there
waiting for someone to find it
and cherish and enjoy its beauty.

∾ ∾

I imagined a young Hispanic woman
named Anna Maria,
mother of five young children
and housekeeper at the hotel
near the museum,
surreptitiously opening the bag
and instantly falling in love
with the purple petunia print,
taking it home to the squalor
of her apartment where it becomes
her precious Flower of Hope
amid the pain she faces daily
when her husband takes out
his drunken rages on her delicate body.
Anna Maria doesn't know
who Georgia O'Keefe was,
but she intuits her spirit
from the purple beauty of the flower
which soothes her wounded body
in places the same color as the print.
When her husband knocks her down
and beats her bloody a final time,
the nurse at the emergency room
doesn't understand the significance
of her faint last words, "Petunia."
But she does note the peaceful smile
on her bruised face as she dies.

∾ ∾

In real life I recall
another purposeful leaving,
this time of uneaten food.
My son takes the container
of my leftover Italian dinner
from a San Francisco restaurant
and puts it down on top of a mail box
for a homeless man or woman
to pick up and enjoy.

∞ ∞

Then I imagined another scene.
Juan Jesus, Anna Maria's husband,
after his release from prison,
ends up years later homeless
on the streets of San Francisco,
grateful for the square white box
filled with shrimp in angel hair
he finds one night
on top of a mail box.

∞ ∞

Whether food for the soul
or food for the body,
to give of oneself
accidentally or purposefully,
unconsciously or consciously,
brings at least momentary sustenance
physically or emotionally
in truth or in fiction.

Can we ever fully know
how much our small acts
of kindness help others?

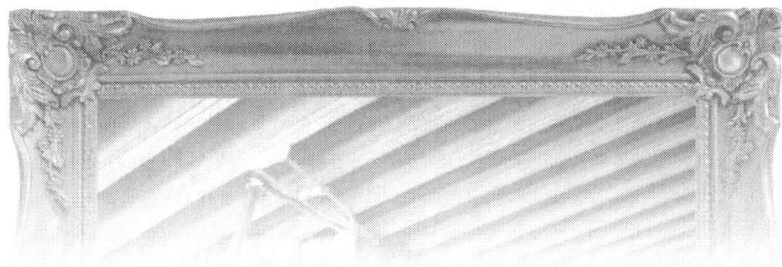

An Early Fall Dance

Solo.
Silent.
Fluttering.
Swirling.
Turning and turning.

These gracefully falling leaves
in shades of avocado,
lemon and tangerine
know how to sway
to the music of the spheres
as they flow, flow, flow
                    down,
                            down,
                                    down,
                                            down.

                                To be crunched
                                and munched
                                and smashed
                                under foot and tire
                                and many rain drops
                                when the music stops
                                at the conclusion
                                of their lovely dance
                                through the cool air.

Life. Love. Joy. Peace.

What is Life
But the living of it?.
A Way of Awakening.
A Dawn.
We wander far from ourselves.
Only to find it there
In us all along.

What is Love
But the accepting of it?
A Way of Cherishing.
A Caress.
We search for it far and wide.
Only to realize finally
We must give it to ourselves
Before we can share it.

What is Joy
But the glorying in it?
A Way of Flying.
A Bird.
We search for it but
It so often eludes us.
It's just around the corner
On our back step all the while.

What is Peace
But the relishing of it?
A Way of Thankfulness.
A Warmth.
We wander looking the world for it.
Only to find it hidden deep
Within us all our days.

What is Heaven
But the glorying in it?
A Wave of Happiness.
An Orgasm.
We expect it in the Other World.
Only to find it fleetingly
Within our hearts and souls here.

Part IV

Dancing the Dream of Life

Speak To Me Tonight

I Want To Incubate
A Dream Tonight.
Ask My Inner Self
What I Need Most
To Do To Be
To Become.

Formally,
Directly
Outrightly,
I Ask,
"Dearest, Deepest
Self Of My Self,
Tell Me
Show Me
Lead Me
Speak Me
Tonight.

Asleep Awake
Awake Asleep

Tonight!

Published In <u>Dream Network Journal</u> 1995

In Transition

Between having and losing.
Between saying goodbye and smiling hellos.
Between living as a couple and living alone.
Between being spoiled and doing everything on my own.
Between having only sons and enjoying a granddaughter.
Between going their way and moving into My Way.

Insight

In and out doors
On and off floors

Through the lights of the night
to "out of sights" in the daylight

Insights delight
Hindsights teach

Both beach us
on inner lakes of awareness

watering the buds and blooms
of our new growths.

To Realms Beyond

"Whoever you are, no matter how lonely,
the world offers itself to your imagination."
Mary Oliver

in another time and place
in another body and soul
what would that mean?

in another universe
on a different planet
what would that be like?

to be outside time
to be without space
could that be possible?

constraints are chains
binding us to the now and here
why can't we let our imagination
let us go wherever whenever?

My Daydreams, AH!

"I broke away
and watched until
I swayed like a wave
between the life
I dreamed and the changing
dream I lived."
Sam Hazo

Torch Singer -
svelte and sexy
deep melodious sounds
assuaging universal suffering

Swan diver -
graceful dancer through the sky
into the mysterious waiting waters
glorying in flight

Famous Writer/Poet/Speaker -
voice for those who are mute
in mind or body or soul
expressing timeless thoughts

Pilot -
high on life and living
grounded in the blue above
flying on the ground below

President of a Human Services Company -
upbeat facilitator
a woman's woman and a man's man
inspiring creative leadership

Founder of a Co-ed Religious Community -
serene and saintly witness
to the anima/animus in all
willing to rescue and uphold

Actress -
down home and warm
versatile and vivacious
performing against the edge of despair

Married Woman Priest -
sensitive to the needs of all the poor
minister to the Communion of Saints
standing tall unique among men

My Daydreams, AH!

During the Interims

"Still achieving, still pursuing,
Learn to labor and to wait."
Longfellow from "The Psalm of Life"

Like farmers planting their fields
hoping the weather will cooperate
until they can bring in a great harvest.

Like pregnant women sheltering their unborns
praying all will go and be well
when they decide to come into this world.

Like investors handing over their money
trusting the Stock Market will advance
so they can make a substantial profit.

Writers, too, must keep on keeping on
creating, writing, publishing
learning "to labor and to wait."

Aren't Longfellow's words
Advice To Live By for all of us?

Dancing the Dream of Life

"I dream you have the courage to dance it all."
Jean Houston

Dancing, dancing, dancing
round and round I go
where I stop
I only know.

Dancing, dancing, dancing
on the wings of the morning,
on the waves of the night.

Dancing, dancing, dancing
to the sound of trumpets,
to the melodies of Cole Porter.

Dancing, dancing, dancing
as a teenager at home alone
in front of a large living room mirror.

Dancing, dancing, dancing
in orgasms of relief,
in frenzies of upset.

Dancing, dancing, dancing
in the softness of flowers,
in the caress of breezes.

Dancing, dancing, dancing
in the aroma of lilacs in the summer,
of burning wood in the winter.

Dancing, dancing, dancing -
one with the music of the spheres
and the tears in things.

Singles' Dances

Sometimes fine fun.
Other times debilitating disaster.
The night will always depend
on the assembled men.

Whether they'll dance
even if we ask one of them
or try to talk or act
the least bit sociable.

So we single-crazy-
Hope-Springs-Eternal
Women of a Certain Age
watch and wait
taking action on our own
to leave early or stay late.

Wondering why some men
just stand around
drinking and gawking at us
not even looking interested
in having any fun
or going out on a limb
taking a chance
to ask one of us to dance.

All men are little boys at heart
after all, aren't they?
Wanting - No, needing
to be the Head Honcho.
The Main Boss.
The One who Always Decides.
The One who runs from rejection
like from a rabid dog or grunting hog.

Either we wait them out
or take the night
into our own hands
or rather mouths
asking one of them to dance
running the risk of rejection
on ourselves.

So that infamous Hope
which continues to spring
crazily eternal within us
propels us to venture out again
tomorrow and tomorrow night
watching, wondering, waiting
for that Elusive Someone

who could change our lives
who could take us to the moon and back
who could be our edge against loneliness....
if only for a few minutes twirl across a dance floor.

Clay Kaleidoscope

Becoming one with the gritty chocolate earth.
Rounding it with and in my novice fingers.
Letting the clay grow up or out or around in my hands.

In class as I scoop out more and more clay
from a too thick-to-be-fired vase,
a chalice beautifully emerges,

but as I continue its sides become paper thin
so reluctantly I roll it all back to its original non-form
giving the clay another chance at transformation.

∾ ∿

The image of the kaleidoscope of the clay
keeps coming back to me.

Each time a new form emerges,
it's as though I've turned
the end of the barrel of a kaleidoscope
and a new fascinating design appears.

The clay of ourselves is in our hands;
what we become is as unique as each dazzling circle
of a multicolored glass kaleidoscope.

Transformation emerges from the pinch pots
and coils and slabs of our formation
as we evolve into new beings of wonder and surprise.

With the Camera of My Mind

Developing pictures.
Images of another time.
In other place.
As another self.

Reviewing.
Reliving.
Renewing.
Restorying.

Rescrolling them back
on rewind or replay.
Going down the pathway again
to find the missing links.

Shift perspectives

to:
initials carved into the top of a wooden table
rusty handles on an old bucket
folds in a ribbon for a bow
bent antenna on a cordless phone
"Delete" key on a broken PC
"Made In" sticker on a stuffed animal
pencils wrapped up in a pack
water in a vase of wilting flowers
scratch on a new mirror
butterflies painted on an indoor birdhouse
white cord on a living room lamp
ID number on the side of a used textbook
knot in a wooden wall
minute hand on a clock
removable inner lining of a man's jacket
a balled-up used paper napkin

In the Mists of Monhegan Island
off the Coast of Maine

Watching the fog thickening
into a total enveloping blanket
from the front porch of the Island Inn
perched on the waterfront.
Then over dinner spinning fantastic stories
about a factitious "Jake the Snake,"
a prisoner at the Maine State Prison
a half hour from Port Clyde,
the departure point for the island ferry,
who escapes one day from his job
in the prison woodworking shop and store
by grabbing a stranger-than-fiction
chance-of-a-lifetime opportunity
by hiding out in a chifferobe
sold to a family on Monhegan.
Disappearing there as a castaway
living by hook or crook
on the edges of visibility.

A wandering mystery man
who might even become an island hero
by saving a little girl from drowning.
Maybe eventually writing and painting
or taking off for other shores
as a crew mate on a ship
bound for somewhere else in the green unknown.
Or maybe ending up a bearded hermit
barely existing in one of the abandoned huts
we can see across the bay
without electricity or water or heat.

Would Jake ever chance enjoying
the rocking chairs on the inn's porch
watching the boats, the frolicking puffins

or the people coming off the ferry
wondering if any one of them is on his trail?
Or dare to slip into one of the little art galleries
sprinkled along the dirt paths of the island?

Or would he walk up to see the big school bell
outside the museum on lighthouse hill
or the John Smith plaque near the school?
Or more likely would he scavenger for leftovers
in the garbage cans behind the restaurants
near the tiny general stores on the way?

Would he lie awake at night
especially during his early days on the run
listening to the haunting sounds
of the fog horns in the distance
from his hideout in the bushes
among the small houses
hanging off the edge of the water
or in the one "For Sale"
surrounded by a mass of ship debris
on the rocks by the edge of the shore?

Or would he stay on the cliff side of the island
when the blanket of the fog is pulled away
by the sparkling blue sky of the next day?

The Unknowns on the Walls

I've often wondered how
people from the early part
of the twentieth century
would react if they saw their portraits
hanging on restaurant walls
as part of an olden days decor.

On the wall to my left
at a Kentucky chain restaurant
hangs a portrait of a newborn,
its sex forever neuter,
its parents forever lost.
Near it an elderly bearded man
in a white shirt,
a black round tie
and black jacket
stares out from a frame.
Could he have been related to the baby?

Across the room from my table
on the wall by the faux fireplace
hangs a picture of a young man
apparently from a more recent time
since there's a light blue shading
behind his head and shoulders.
To his right an older couple
stares out at the world from their portrait,
possibly done for their anniversary.
All wear extremely serious expressions
particularly ironic because now here
they're looking down on
a room of joviality and pleasure.

Was it just not the "in" thing
in the last century to smile for a portrait?

Would these people have agreed
to go on display like this
if they had been given a choice?
Aren't these unknowns on restaurant walls
equivalent to the unknown soldier
with no names or history,
all anonymous?

And how would I react a century from now
if one of my photos turned up on a wall?
Disbelief thinking my eyes deceived me.
Irked at being on public display
even if anonymously or especially because so.
Disturbed that no one in my family
saw fit to keep my portrait for posterity
for my grandchildren and great grandchildren
as well as for all the others who would follow me.

Dear Unknowns on the Walls
of whatever establishments,
I suppose you'll never know
you've become such public figures
your portraits are hanging all over town
in places you would least expect to see them.
I'm sorry I'll never know who you were
and what kind of lives you lived.

May you each be at peace wherever you are.

Ballerina Primroses at Dusk

"The night opens the flowers in secret
 and allows the day to get the thanks." Tagore

Silent ballet dancers,
each one in her own rhythm
blooooooms and blooooooms
glorious bright lemon beauty.

In awed fascination
I watch their lovely dance,
Knowing they will hold
First position all night

And die in the morning.

Flowing into the Fog

the pure white ahead

the unknown

seeing nothing

knowing nothing

open to whatever

whenever however

Flowing into the fog

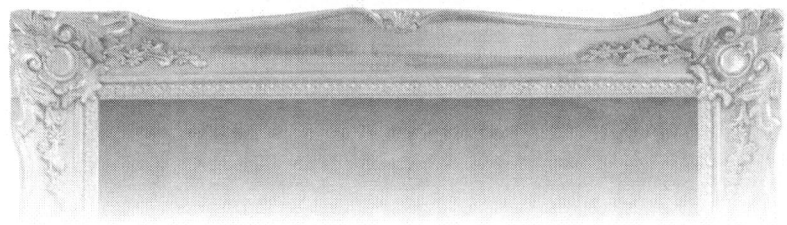

At Sea

Literally.
On the Ms Zuiderdam
of the Holland America cruise line
in the Eastern Caribbean.

Figuratively.
Lost and lonely
among the more than two thousand aboard.
Knowing that ultimately
we're on the way to Nassau.
But not knowing
where I'm really going
during the rest of my days.

Turning sixty-five in a few weeks.
What do I still want to do, to accomplish?
To write, to dance, to laugh, to...

Enjoy life with multiple grandchildren
and even great grandchildren
With awareness and stamina and strength.

At Sea.

With myself and where I'm going.
How to change directions?
Pull up anchor to new places
within and with out of myself.
To explore the depths
of the ocean inside.

To honor what mysteries I find there.
What new species of life unknown to me before.

At Sea.

Exploration.
Discovery.
Decision.
"Knowing when to walk away,
knowing when to run" à la Rogers.

When to drop anchor
and when to speed
full steam ahead.

At Sea.

Wondering what port of myself
I'll pull into next.
What places await me
during the rest of my journey.

Pregnant with Joy

I find out I'm pregnant.
Then Joy tells me something
that I forget after I wake up.
My sense is three things.
But what they are I don't recall.

My unconscious seems to be telling me
I'm pregnant with new life
even in my mid 60's,
and that Joy has something to tell or teach me.
What is it? What three things is Joy telling me?

Actually, it doesn't matter I can't remember them
because my unconscious self does.
They are written on my inner hard drive.
Hopefully, I'll remember them
when the time warrants that I am ready.

"We dance round in a circle and suppose
while the Secret sits in the middle and knows,"
as Robert Frost put it.

Or as Yeats did,
"The Center I cannot find
is known to my unconscious mind."

Pregnant with Joy.
What a wondrous phrase
Or situation.
Or State of Being.
At whatever age.

Dream Queries

Do we dream dreams
or do they dream us?
Do we become the images of our dreams
or do they image us?
Do we speak in our dreams with the tongues of inner prophets
or do they prophesy for us?

Do we traverse on inner oceans of depths beyond understanding
or do we become Oceans instead?
Do we sleep into the answers of our lives
or do the questions awake us?
Do we thrash in the beds of our nightmares
or do our night terrors scare us into action?

Do we get caught up trying to find meaning in our dreams
or do we just let our dreams have meaning?
Do we need to dream every night even if we don't recall anything
or do dreams need our awareness for life?
Do we stop dreaming when we've had enough
or do we just begin to dream at that point?

Do we wish we were more loving, attractive, relaxed, renewed
or
do we ignore our tastes, touches, glimpses into true happiness?

Do we spend our sleep in a haze of incongruous experiences
or
do these same weird events actually wake us up asleep?

Do we wander around in circles on the labyrinth of ourselves
or
do these mazes parallel the complexity of our inner selves?

A Question That Changed
Their Lives

She was sitting at a singles' dance that May night
casually watching people milling around the room
in search of dance partners, listeners or lovers.
All edges against their loneliness,

when she noted a tall attractive black-haired man
walk the length of the long narrow bar
and then wind around and around and around it
in circle after circle past the table where she sat.

She counted the times he walked this same circuit -
One, three, six, eight, ten -
until she couldn't keep quiet any longer
and stopped him to ask the innocent question
which changed their lives and made three other ones possible.
"Do you know you're walking in circles?"

The rest is the hectic history
of their nearly forty years together
walking in circles they never could have imagined
that otherwise ordinary Sunday night so long ago.

Before Getting Pregnant
for the First Time

Watching the riffraff of adolescent humanity
in the school hallway.

The out-of-it alcoholics red-eyed from hangovers,
the free and easy girls bedroom-eyeing the guys,
the myriad non-students with eyes everywhere
except in their books, dusty in their lockers.
She would say to herself,
"Oh my God, is that what I could bring into this world?"

Then making a major LEAP of FAITH
that she would do her best with the ones sent her,
one day she smiled a hello
after a special visit to her doctor
and cried out to her man,

"Hi, Daddy."

My Three Angels
from Manhattan

"Outside the open window
the morning air is all awash with angels."
Richard Wilbur

It was the first week of
August of '86
when I met each of them
though I didn't realize
who they were at the time....

I had just said a sad goodbye
to Don, my "Place Mat Man,"
from Progoff's Intensive Journal Writing Workshop
on the Hudson at Mariandale, New York.
After I got into the city on the train,
I had to leave one station
and go across town to another.
It was raining and I was weighed down
with so many books and bags,
I could hardly manage them.

Standing at the exit of the station in the rain
trying to decide which way to go to the bus
and how to carry all my things while holding an umbrella,
a handsome man beside me offered to help.
He carried one of my bags,
held an umbrella over my head
and even gave me the exact change
for the bus a block away
before he disappeared
leaving me waiting for it on the corner.

I barely made it through the door
of the Grand Central Station
when all my books and papers in my arms
cascaded across the floor.
Before I could bend down to try to retrieve them,
a man "flew" out of the Parimutuel Betting Office
across the way to help me.

He like the other man carried my bags,
this time across the station,
telling me he was only in New York
during this one week of the year
to reestablish his citizenship here.

Then before I could thank him,
he, too, disappeared into the crowds.

(Several years later back in Grand Central Station,
I noticed a large sign warning visitors against letting
anyone carry their bags in the complex
and I wondered whom my two angels were helping now.)

When my train was called,
I faced the arduous task
of lugging all my things
down a steep pair of stairs.
No one - man or woman or angel -
came to my assistance this time.
So I almost fell into the train
and into the first empty seat.
There beside me by the window
sat a well dressed man
whose glasses I almost smashed
when I plopped down relieved.
I smiled "Sorry!" and looked into the eyes
of a person to whom I knew I could bare my soul.

For the next few hours that's exactly what I did.
Though he was a Captive Audience of One,
I never once felt he didn't want to listen
or was put out hearing the story
of my just past wondrous week on the Hudson.
As we talked he helped me put my week
of becoming closely connected to Don and Life renewed
and especially myself into a wider perspective.
He had just been wined, dined and honored, so he told me,
in Manhattan for his outstanding business accomplishments.
When he got up to leave the train and my life,
I was led to put my hand on his cheek
and caress his soft black beard.
At that moment I somehow "knew"
he really was from another "place."

I think back today a decade or so later
to those few special hours in the city and on the train,
convinced that the three men who "flew" to my aid
really were My Three Manhattan Angels.

Postscript in Life as it continues:
My third angel did give me his name
and the place where he worked in the area,
but when I called they had never heard of him.

Sea Gulls at Dinner on Long Island Sound

Backing away,
I watch them.

Human curiosity
fearing invasion of privacy.
Retaliation.

Sleek white and black
water beauties at dinner.

Heads of four fish
and eaten-away bodies remain
on the beach table.

One still hungry bird
swoops onto another at meal.

Survival.
Its fight everywhere.

I watch them.

Part V

Isle of Lore: Ireland

Mizen Head

Waves crashing
Winds howling
at this southernmost point
of Ireland
in the Atlantic.

Wondering if,
as the story goes,
three Irish brothers,
my husband's ancestors,
really stood near here
or perhaps at Queenstown
before leaving home around 1600
for the streets of gold
in the semi-mythical America.

Now hundreds of years later
my three sons
are their descendants.
The oldest standing with me
at the lighthouse
in the raging 70 mph gales.

Holding on to each other,
holding up against the winds.

On Visiting Poet John O'Donohue's Grave

As I watch a man kneel and pray
at the grave site of his inspiration,
role model and friend,
John's words stream through my soul,
"May all that is unlived in you
Blossom into a future
Graced with love."

To which I respond again with his words,
"May I live this day
Compassionate of heart, clear in word,
Gracious in awareness,
Courageous in thought,
Generous in love."

Thank you, John.
Your thoughts parallel
the ones in the prayer
I've been saying
since I was fifteen,
Whatever You want me to be,
I will be.
Give me the courage,
the strength,
the unselfishness,
but especially
the superabundance of love.

Today I pray further
for heightened
discernment and discovery
on all the paths
I am destined to walk
during the reminder
of my days.

On Hearing Note One
of Sean Costello singing "Leaving Liverpool"

"Farewell to you, my own true love,
I am going far away....
I know it will be a long long time
till I see your lovely face again...."

I am mesmerized,
bedazzled,
blown away
and stunned
as gushing tears
cascade down my shirt.
The music of Sean's soul
seeps deep into mine
as I imagine he's my husband
saying goodbye to me
two years ago.

Still I could have
run off into the sunset
with this handsome Irish tenor
on the stage in Galway,
even though he could be my son
and no surprise is married.

Nevertheless,
in a parallel universe
beyond earthly constraints,
we are coupled together
by song, emotion
and passion.

The Weight of the Words

Standing against each of the stone pillars in turn
at the entrance of the Writers' Museum,
a restored Georgian mansion on Parnell Square in Dublin.

Trying to let the solid firmness permeate my being
with the words, the wonder, the creative prowess
of all and each of the writers of Ireland.

Among them Joyce (I bought his Ulysses in the bookstore.)
And of course Yeats, Shaw, Wilde, Swift, Sheridan
and so many others known and not so known.

Four Nobel Prizes in the group, especially Beckett's in '69,
the year I completed my MA thesis on his "Waiting for Godot"
with my subtitle, "Man's Search for Meaning in Absurdity."

Photos of Stone Stairs
up to Wherever

Thinking about the attics of ourselves.
What is hidden there?
What are we meant to find there
at the end of our climb?
What mysteries of Life lay
in waiting for us
in that cluttered space
at the top of our minds?

Ah, the Stairs to the Attic.
I step up and up and up
while at the same time
go down and down
into the core of myself.
Oxymoron of awareness.
Of discernment.
Of discovery.
All hiding inside myself.

I fly high yet dive deep.
I climb the highest mountain
and walk on the bottom of the Atlantic.
I sit among the stars
while I lounge inside the hollow earth.
I curl up in the clouds
yet swim on the backs of whales.
I soar on the wings of angels
as I sink into the ground of my being.
I become a tiny daisy in the soft grass
and a towering stone ruin of a castle.

I smell all there is to smell.
Taste all of it
touching everything
that can be touched.
Seeing the whole universe
in a vivid double rainbow,
I listen to the songs of the saints.

Ruins at Newgrange and Knowth

5000 years of stone set in place
so no rain can penetrate the space.
Minds undoubtedly intelligent
beyond classrooms
and PhD's and awards.
Sun and moon lines
light their darkness.

What must it have been like?
How much of a life
filled their years?
Without books.
Electricity.
Facebook.
Or anything we take
for granted every day.

Just basic survival
yet so much more.
Endurance.
Stamina.
Acumen.
The Celtic Spirit
of wonder and Joy.

May I emulate
some tiny piece
of their fortitude,
their strength,
their zest for Life.

Reconnecting with a Favorite Poet While Visiting His Homeland:
My Lake Isle Innisfree à la W. B. Yeats

I relish my peace here
at my "Silver Spur B&B"
above a lake in Western Maryland.
A peace that "comes dropping slow"
since my husband's death two years ago.
A peace "dropping from the veils of morning"
to midnight's "glimmer' and noon's "glow."

I feel Ed in this place as I recall his answer
to a whiteboard question in his ICU room
the week before he left me and our sons,
"What do you do in your leisure time?"
And I hear his response
in my "deep heart's core,"
"Relax at Deep Creek Lake."

But now his face is hidden from me
"amid a cloud of stars."

The Joys of Discovery
Meeting New Friends

Brainwave alignments.
Personal is Universe connections.
Dream synchronicities.

Fun on the Run.
Talk on the Walk.
Laugh on the Path.

All in Together Now,
my new Forever Friends!

Across the Middle of Ireland

Glorying in:

blankets of meadows
green and glowing

mountain sides divided by
enduring limestone fences

radiant rainbows
against sunny dark skies

ewe's backsides painted various colors
depending on how long pregnant

many small town pubs
fields of cows black and brown

remnants of enormous mounds
evidence of long ago intelligence

all the while leaning
up against a wall of warm stone

as the afternoon sun shines
on it from a right angle

a quiet beach
a moment of contemplation.

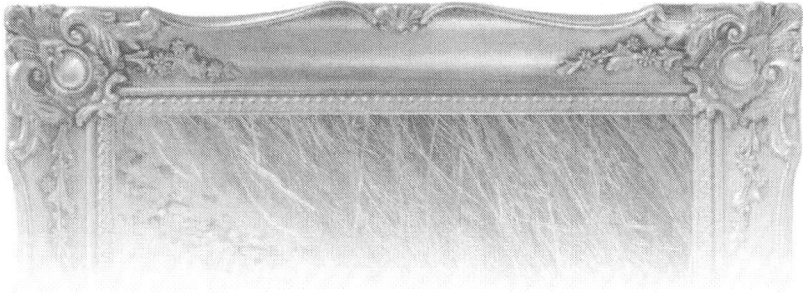

A Senior Mother Moment

On a bus in Cork, Ireland
fifteen minutes
from a beach visit,
all of a sudden
in panic mode,
I jump up and cry out,
"Martin, stop the bus!
My son's not here!"

I had looked behind me,
but he wasn't in his usual seat,
I therefore believed
he had been left behind
photographing.

Ah, Relief of Reliefs,
when he called out,
"Here I am, Mom!"
On the bus he was
the entire time.

Only a few fleeting moments
in panic mode.

In Transit - Dublin to Newark

almost home
but we always
take ourselves
with us
wherever we go -
our good,
bad or
ugly selves

for me
my renewed self
from this Pilgrimage
these past two weeks
new friends
new insights
new experiences
ruins, churches,
cemeteries, monasteries
and new appreciation
for the Celtic Church

so I will cherish
these gifts
chez moi
with my family
and old friends
holding them close
to my Yeats' "heart's core"

with copious thanks
every dawn and dusk
to "My Main Man"
who has made me all I am
and meant to be and become

My Meditation Chair

Is actually a swing hanging
from the ceiling in my office
at my mountain home
installed significantly
two days after returning
from my journey
to the famed Emerald Isle.

I can watch the sunrise
over the water while sitting on it
and see the lake itself
through the trees.
I can swing in a full circle
or just back and forth.

The blue bird sitting on a limb
surrounded by fuchsia-colored flowers
will be my inspiration here
and in my mind's eye wherever else
for continued prayer and creativity
exuding from my halcyon retreat
across the Atlantic

Part VI

And The Flow Continues

Three Weeks

It's been three weeks since
I got the news.

It's been three weeks since
I traveled eight hours across two states.

It's been three weeks since
I drove through The Lord's Valley

near Promised Land State Park
and the Blooming Grove.

It's been three weeks since
I listened to Marian Woodman's twelve tapes

as I drove through double tunnels
named Blue Mountain and Kittanning
with only several car lengths between the two.

It's been three weeks since
I realized their significance
as Birth Canal. Life. Death Canal.

It's been three weeks since
My sisters and I picked out her casket.

Yes, it's been only three weeks since
we laid our Mom to rest
on a sunny July afternoon
on a hill overlooking a city and a river
with a majestic mountain
standing guard in the distance.

The Tears of Things

"I remember reading how in ancient times
the Chinese nobles saved in sealed jars
every tear they'd ever shed." Barbara Bloom

If I had ever tried to imitate these men,
I would have been sorely tested
even if I only saved the insignificant tears
like the ones I shed from a novel I recently read.
Or the ones from a hurtful name
a student called me in anger.
Or others from an antiseptic applied to a wound.
Or from ones as a off shoot of my extreme sensitivity
because a boss shook his head angrily at me.

Or ones gushing from deeper inside me
like my Holy Hour tears every Saturday night
when I was all of twenty something.
Tears that should have told me I didn't belong
in the convent I had chosen to enter at eighteen.

Then there were the bigger tears
cascading down my reddened face
when a doctor yells at me over the phone
because I hadn't called him in an emergency
but simply for his reassurance
about my husband's condition.
Tears I had to swallow
to be able to teach my next class
only a few minutes later.

Or my gushing tears of overwhelming joy
at the wedding of the first of my three sons
when I knew both Mom and Dad were there
and could feel each of them for fleeting seconds

happy for all of us from the Other Side.
These tears of joy surpassed the ones
that had swept down my face
when I heard they died years before.

Oh, there's no way I can remember
all the many tears of my life.
I only know that if I had tried
to follow in the path
of the ancient nobles of China,
there wouldn't have been
enough sealed jars to save them in.

A Sonnet to a Snowy March Day

This morning snow just covers roofs with white
as tiny flakes continue to fall and fall.
Soon Spring with all her glory will alight
on ground on tree on bush in hearts and all.

Good bye to cold and snow and all things ice
they had their run but now must go away
since sun and warm and buds will now suffice
to bring us hope and peace with each blue day.

I welcome Spring with open arms' laughter
Spring brings new life new hope new love in deeds
I'll fly and dance in the now and after
on wings of birds on stems of trees in seeds.

La Nuit

The night speaks,
Whispers
A Promise.

"It's time...
Time for forgetting.
Go away with me.
I am your Dream."

Published In <u>Dream Network Journal</u> 1995

In the Still of the Night at Deep Creek Lake

I ponder the mysteries of life.
Where I've come from.
Where I'm going.
How I'll get there
wherever it is.

Knowing that as I ponder
the earth keeps spinning
effortlessly beyond me
and the stars shower beauty
across the blue canvas
of the night sky.

Soon I will close my eyes
to sleep and to dream
of wondrous new tomorrows
with adventures yet to be lived.

As time and space
envelop me
in their waiting arms
and I sink into the deep waters
of my unconscious self.

My Sleeping Self Speaks

"I want the one rapture of an inspiration." Gerard Manley
Hopkins

"Go back to the womb.
Take it easy.
Be kind to yourself.
Slow down.
Curry favor."

"I LOVE YOU."

"You are very lucky!"
"You have not lost it!"

"It's great to be 50."

As Marion Goodman's brother said,
"The sh-t is in the hands of God."
To this my sleeping self advises,
"So err on the side of being human."

Then and Now

"We carry our childhood in our arms."
Linda Pastan

Then: Circa Fifty Years Ago
Standing in our small white picket fenced front yard
fantasizing flying in a silver bird in the sky.

Solving crimes with Nancy Drew.
Laughing with Uncle Milty.

Beating down the "jungle" vegetation with my sister
on the way to "our" blackberry patch.

Horseback riding high on a friend's two wheel bike
into the Wild West of my imagination.

(I wasn't allowed to have a bike of my own
since we lived at the bottom of a hill.)

Playing house with my best friend, Barb and Lois,
in the log cabin my father built in Lois' yard.

Shaping stones with them
on the curb in front of 205 James.

Wondering all the while
what I'd be when I grew up.

Now: The Twenty-first Century

Flying out into worlds of the future through sci-fi classics
like 1984, Fahrenheit 451, and Brave New World.

Reveling in the ever amazing and surprising
worlds of my dreams and fantasies.

Now being the little girl I never really was Then.
Today playing Real House and having Real Baby Dolls.

Enjoying coloring and painting again
or simply acting crazy with my family.

Talking and singing in my own unique language
which even my grown sons imitate.

Making up jokes and laughing in great joy.
Now so different from the shy girl of my youth.

As only my mother used to be able to testify,
having left her fun-loving self here in me

that unforgettable July day in 2001
as her Spirit waltzed and polkaed into the next world...

A Reason Still Here?

Something else I am to accomplish?
Someone else I am to help?
Something else I'm supposed to....?

A huge tree limb
hit by lightening
two days before
smolders on the tree
and within hours
of my walking
up the driveway
where it would fall,
it topples over
but not hurting me
or the mail man
or whoever could
have just been there.

Almost eight years
to the day
when my car
hydroplaned
and smashed into
a guard fence,
not just a rail,
virtually uninjured
the car destroyed.

That was about forty years
after the night
as a brand new nun,
I walked into the complete dark
of the hall outside
the college pool

searching for the light switch
as I patted along the wall,
feeling a door knob
that turned and opened
hearing words loud and clear,
"Do not take a step."

Which I didn't…
when I flicked the light on,
I realized I was standing
at the top of the stairs
leading to the ominous concrete floor
of the boiler room.

I am still here
for some reason.
Some purpose.
At nineteen in the convent
to stay until thirty
marry at thirty-five
have my first son the next year
and then my twin sons
twenty-two months later.

And now since I left
the full-time classroom
only a month before
my car hydroplaned,
is it to work with all
the home instruction students
mostly new teenage moms
and just this past week
to know again
there is a reason
for me to still be here
to teach, to tutor,
to counsel, to listen,
to help, to direct,

to be whoever I am to be
to whoever I am to meet
and connect with
and be of help to?

Yes, there's no doubt I'm still here
to "live along into the answer,"
as Rilke once wrote to a young poet.

Leaving Home and Letting Go

"To live in this world
you must be able
to do three things:
to love what is mortal;
to hold it
against your bones knowing
your own life depends on it;
and, when the time comes to let it go,
to let it go."
Mary Oliver from "In Blackwater Woods"

My oldest son left for college today
at the university in the next town
just twenty minutes from our house.
Still I couldn't hold back tears
as I hugged him good-bye in his dorm.
He'll be eighteen in two months.

And I remembered my leaving home
three weeks after I turned eighteen
to enter the convent an hour away
from my home in a small town,
though really another world away.

Imagining seeing my new self as my mother did
as I came down the wide marble stairs
in the front hall of the Motherhouse
shrouded in black from head to toe,
her oldest daughter another person
in a strange world with strangers.

And I could only guess
how difficult it must have been
for my mother to say good-bye to me
believing she would never see me again,

at least not as a regular person,
though she did a dozen years later when I left
and married and had three sons in two years.

Yet her grandmother had faced the worst
of all these leavings, these letting go's,
when her seventeen year old daughter
at the turn of the century
left her home on a farm
in Hungary outside Budapest
for a new life many worlds away
in Braddock, Pennsylvania.

Never going home again though years later
her husband, also a native Hungarian,
had the money from two businesses he owned:
a swimming pool and a coal mine
before the Depression took everything
including their way ever to go home again,
ever to see their family and friends
and their home country once more.

Who's to say which mother actually had it harder?
For each and all the good-bye was GOOD-BYE.
The flesh of her flesh and bone of her bone
would never be home again in the same way
no matter what or how or when.
No matter if her son or daughter
ever walked in the house again,
ever came to dinner on a holiday
or ever stayed the night again.
NO, IT WOULD NEVER BE THE SAME.

Still and all I can't help believing
it had to be the hardest for my great-grandmother
to say good-bye to my grandmother-to-be.
There was a finality in their leave taking
which went beyond time and space.

As I say to my high school students today,
it would be like their leaving their families
for Mars and never going home again.

One day before she died
Grandma told her youngest daughter
that the day she left her family
she knew she would never go home again.

Did her mother know as well?

Published in the <u>Mercy Newsletter</u> October 1995, p.16

An Autobiography in Miniature:
How Intuition Announces Itself
Literally or Figuratively
in Body or Spirit

Having a sense
an inkling or flash of insight
that something's about to happen.

Getting an abrupt, out-of-the-blue
brainstorm to do something
to go out on a limb.

Feeling a pain or a jolt
in the pit of my stomach
for no apparent physical reason.

Breaking out in goose bumps
with a sudden shiver
heightening the senses.

Just "knowing" to do
or not to do something
at a certain time.

Hearing an inner voice
saying to do or not to do,
to go or not to go.

#1:
Ahead of time but without a decision made,
I "knew" that the Christmas of '56
was to be my last one at home.
I lived that long ago holiday season
with that awareness telling no soul of my plans
to become a nun after high school graduation.
Living as though with multiple personalities:

my seventeen year old fun-loving high school senior self
and my idealistic, ready to sacrifice my all religious self.
Actually, I did enter the convent
on September 7 of the next year.

#2:
I "knew" weeks before an August '69
Communication Workshop in St. Louis
that it was going to be very significant
so much so that I wrote a series of postcards
to my special friends at the time
asking them to pray for me.
Actually, this workshop led to my key experience
of "Birth" at thirty the next month
and subsequently to my decision
to leave the convent that Fall.

#3:
I "knew" in early January '70
when I went to inform the Mother General
that I had decided to leave
that she would say if you're that sure,
leave at semester break at the end of the month.
So I asked a priest friend ahead of time
if she could make me leave then.
He assured me I could call all my own shots.
Actually, she did tell me to go at semester break,
but I insisted I had a commitment to the school
where I had been teaching,
so I left on June 7th at the end of the semester.

#4:
I "knew" the summer of '74
was to be my last one as a single woman.
So on the spur of the last moment
at the beginning of summer vacation from teaching,
I booked a flight to Martinique
for a week's stint at Club Med.

Later that year Ed and I became
quite serious about each other.
Actually, we were engaged at Christmas
and married on the first day of Spring the next year.

#5:
I "knew" I was carrying twins
when my waist grew five inches
during a week's holiday
in Key West in February of '78.
When I felt different from my other pregnancy
several years before with my first son.
When I continued to expand
like a Happy Birthday balloon.
When I stretched out on the sonogram table
at five months pregnant.
Actually, in August '78 the day before my thirty-ninth birthday,
I delivered twin sons by natural childbirth
Brendan at 11 pm and Patrick fifty minutes later.
Ed and I celebrated their births and my birthday
over orange juice in the recovery room.

#6:
I "knew" in November of '96
while sitting in my friend Natalie's kitchen
that I had to leave the full-time classroom.
I felt the same gut sensation
as I did when I knew I had to leave the convent.
I lived into the full realization
through many concerns about money.
Actually, I left teaching in June '97 with no regrets.
Never looking back after thirty-five years straight.
Now with a coast all clear to the future.

Oh, Intuition, you remain my Special Inner Guide
to decisions and change and New Life.

Full Moon and Empty Arms

at Refugium Restaurant
outside on a square
our last night in Berlin
September 24, 2010

A memorable evening an understatement.
A waitress covers my shoulders
with a peach fleece wrap
as I enjoy a fine German meal
of pork knuckles and sauerkraut
at one of the city's best restaurants.
A cool breeze whispers
and a cool sax warbles
as the full moon shines edged in white
between two ornate buildings.

I'm traveling with my oldest son
not my husband his father
now a year dead.
Live sax music out on the square
regular and alto with accompaniment
stirs me to tears with familiar songs.

La Vie en Rose
My Way
Mona Lisa
My Heart Belongs to Daddy
Raindrops Keep Falling

In my mind and somewhat out loud
I croon "Full Moon and Empty Arms"
(Kay and Mossman '45)
frequently sung by Sinatra

"Full moon and empty arms
tonight I use the magic moon
to wish upon
and next full moon
if my one wish comes true
my empty arms will be filled by you."

Wearing my heart on my sleeve,
I'm still teary eyed when we get up to leave.
Missing Ed so much and a new friend as well,
I feel alone with the full moon and empty arms.

Almost Full Circle

"We do not cease being women because the blood or the milk no
longer flows from our bodies. If anything we are more complete
women. We have tread almost full circle."
Patricia Garfield

Having just turned fifty-five,
considered a senior citizen now by some,
though certainly not by me...yet,
I flow now more than I did when I flowed.

For me one of the greatest things
about getting older is perspective.
On my way from DC to Boston recently,
before the plane soared above the clouds
I could see how all the roads
crossed and connected
leading from way to way.

Getting older means I have this perspective
I didn't have at twenty or thirty or even forty
so I can see how the paths and bypasses,
super highways and dead ends of my life
are all part of an increasingly completed puzzle
of my life as it evolves.

I know now why that love affair
I really longed for with all my heart and soul
didn't work out.
And why the "Love of My Life" could never
bring me COMPLETE fulfillment.
Why I didn't get that "perfect" job,
or suffered under an insensitive nitpicking boss.

I flow now more than I did when I flowed.

Our physical streams dried up,
we evolve into fine rivers
of love and joy and understanding,
realizing the foibles and fantasies
of our lives are played over and over again
in different ways in the lives of the people we meet.

We no longer think we're weird or strange
because we felt or did differently
than our peer group in the past.

Now "we do what we want to do
when we want to do it,"
as an old friend now in her eighties
told me in her "sexy sixties."
Intent on pleasing ourselves
and giving ourselves what we need,
we only harbor minor concern or interest
in what other people think
or do or don't do.

Secure within ourselves,
we embrace the tides of change,
slowing down sometimes
while speeding up at others.
At the same time glorying in the gifts
we've always known we had
but never truly honored.

The road ahead to whatever is waiting
in the rest of our lives
is filled with turnoffs,
winding paths and dead ends
but, most of all, with marvelous way stations
where we will continue to grow and become.
Hopefully, all we woman of a "certain age"
flow now more than we did when we flowed.

Room 223

Leaving my last classroom
after thirty-five years
attempting to teach teenagers
writing, literature and life.

My first classroom
three and a half decades ago
was in another state
both geographically and by vow.

I was a young nun then
in that old building
called Epiphany Elementary School
in an area later to be known as
Inner City Pittsburgh, Pennsylvania.

Shrouded in a floor length pleated black serge habit.
Heavy starched cloth surrounding my face
and digging into my twenty-two year old forehead
as well as across my virginal breast.
Confining my loving-to-dance feet,
black old lady Cuban heeled oxfords with strings,
the kind in fashion now for teenage girls
which I would never wear again today.

Just thinking yesterday
that for full circle closure
I would put an ad
in the Pittsburgh Press
to try to locate Lorraine,
my main bright light that year,
in my maiden class - a seventh grade.
Today she and her peers
would be almost fifty!
How can that be?

Little Larry a half century old as well?
He who every day at dismissal
as he tumbled down the three flights,
would look up at me with his Dennis the Menace eyes
and squeal, "Night, Sister. Have a good weekend!"
Where is he now?
He might even be a grandfather today.

And what about Linda,
a tomboy at that time,
who gave me all kinds of flack,
where is she today?

It's significant
that the only roll of photos
that I have of any
of my former students
is the one of this class,
with the thirteen year olds
who'd be all grown up now
or even "out of here" already.

Where have all the years gone
long time passing?
Where have all the many thousands
who have succeeded or failed
in and out of my classrooms gone
long time ago?

Dream Why Not's?
POURQUOI PAS?

What if we could retrieve past dreams
ones long or recently forgotten at will?

What if we could retrieve key ones
dreamt before major decisions or events
historic or personal
experienced by ourselves or other key persons?

What if we could dream the future?

What if we could dream ways to change
hard situations or impossible ones?

What would we become if we really honored
the awarenesses from all our dreams?

What if we could really and easily
program, incubate, determine dreams we need
even if we don't realize we need them?

How much do we know unconsciously
or subconsciously at any one point?

Can we lead, train, inspire
our unconscious and subconscious
to communicate directly with our conscious selves?

Can we consciously program dream cures,
dream resolutions to problems,
answers to questions
release from stress?

What if we could use hypnosis -
self or professionally induced -
to remember all our dreams
or simply selected ones on certain nights
kind of a take off on Wilder's play Our Town
when Emily returns to her twelfth birthday
- a waking dream or was it a nightmare
after the birth of her second child?

What if there were an easy surefire way
to return to a great dream
or an unresolved one?

What if on demand we could live
in this alternate universe not just in memory
but in a way in fact to get beyond
or to survive terrible pain?

What if we could engineer a real life
for the wisdom figures
or wonderful strangers of our dreams,
i.e. my handsome blond from my dream in '86
to be like an imaginary adult playmate?

What if? Why not? When? Now? Already? Fine!
Pourquoi pas?

Into the Void

Overlooking the Pacific Ocean
July 15, 1999

All is a luminous blanket beyond my retreat room garden.
All is an alabaster spread stretched out before me.
All is a silver shroud of fog obliterating ocean and sky
Merging them in a oneness of awed beauty
I am nearly breathless to describe.

What lies beyond this time and place,
I cannot now know.
But I am willing to throw myself
into the arms of my God
in the mist enveloping all.

He will guide me through it and beyond it
helping me face the uncertainties of my life.
He will uncover the covered places
making known to me his paths
from this day forward.

Yes, I Bless Them!

"....bless the images
that stalk the corners of our sights
and will not let go."
2011 Poet Laureate Philip Levine

My Dad on the telephone
tears pouring down his face
as he tells family and friends
he has a son finally.
I'm nine, the oldest
of his three daughters.

My Mom putting a lone rose
on my Dad's coffin
then kneeling down to pray.
I'm barely forty with
three sons under five.

My husband shaking his head "NO"
when our oldest son asked
if he was going to be OK
less than a week before he died
two years ago next month.

So many more images
too many to put into words
"stalk the corners of (my) sights"
this sunny August morning.

Still I don't want any of them to leave me.

Love Is...

Love is
a tear, a smile and a warm hug.

Love is
sharing and questioning and honoring
and holding on tight to each other in the dark.

Love is
anticipation, satisfaction,
distraction and clarification,
all wrapped up in a Ball of Wonder.

Love is
being there for, missing when away,
running toward and hanging in together
in every challenge.

Love is
friendship, compassion,
understanding and acceptance
each and all to the Nth degree.

Love is
a taste, a touch,
a birdsong of Heaven in the Wings.

Love is
a Joy of Joys,
a Gift of Gifts,
the best reason to keep on keeping on
no matter what.

Toward a Global Ethic for the 21st Century and Beyond

(Read and on display at a Global Ethic Expo at New Harmony, Indiana, the first week of May 1998)

We acknowledge
interdependence.

We embrace
diversity.

We applaud
individuality.

Yet we also honor
universality.

We reach out
to all cultures
to all religions
to all races.

We glory in the colors of a global ethic.
A kaleidoscope of an ethic for the earth.

A global kaleidoscope
of changing colors and patterns.

A mosaic ever evolving.
Ever transforming.

With the colors of the dawn and the dusk
and all the shades in between intermingled.

We marvel at the beauty of the change:
the realignment

the rearrangement
the renewing
of peoples and beliefs,
understandings and revelations,
concerns and connections,
constraints and conflicts.

All in constant flux.
Tides in and tides out.
Ever surging as the ocean.
Water and salt and big fish and little.

Hair, Curves and Shadows

Three "over the hill" people pull
into a ribs restaurant in Rehobeth, Maryland.

One sits a the wheel of his Chevy beforehand
hairspraying his "manicured" hair.

The other sports a mop of slicked back black hair
formed into a DA right out of the 50's.

The third's flat listless brown hair
is five o'clock splashed across his face.

As these three of the masculine persuasion
move off to the right from the parking lot,

a Ford with three "dog" women
jerks into a space next to their car.

The driver wearing a too tight purple top
displaying multiple rolls of fat above her waist.

The woman riding shotgun, stern and masculine,
she has no distinguishing curves on her body.

The third a nondescript shadow of a person
the kind no one remembers, a fader into the woodwork.

Are they all off to the same party
or were they set up to meet each other?

Will any of them "get lucky" tonight
or will they all go home to empty apartments
alone again?

The overweight woman to devour a pint of chocolate ice cream.
The mannish woman to read an entire Sports Illustrated.
The shadow woman to fantasize about being Betty Davis.

The manicured man to sit peering at himself in a vanity mirror.
The lackluster man to sit for hours staring into space.
The fifties rerun man to listen to Oldies on a vintage radio.

Each of them still living lonely Eleanor Rigby lives.

In the Midst
of a Maryland Winter

when snow and ice
are hazards to foot and tire,

when days are dark and foreboding
and nights raspingly cold,

I will remember Logos
perched on the edge of the Santa Lucias.

In the midst of a Maryland winter,

when I'm feeling depressed and downhearted
because nothing I do seems enough,

when I rant and rage against the elements
more inside me than out far too often,

I'll rush my mind back to this place of peace
and sit on the porch again in the morning,

feeling the sun burn the haze over the ocean
awakening the rippling water to blue.

In the midst of a Maryland winter,

when I yearn for peace among the hassles of every day
because nothing seems to go right no matter how hard I try,

when the cold on the outside
out degrees what I feel inside,

I'll smile and remember the warmth of my friends here,
their caring and concern and compassion,

and pray with the monks in the Chapel
knowing they are all my brothers.

In the Midst of a Maryland Winter,

I'll return to a trailer called Logos
above the Pacific Ocean at Big Sur.

Contrails

a wide series of contrails
across the Pacific sky of Big Sur
lines of several jets
intersect as though
to crash in the air
looking like long squiggly white lines
a child might have sprawled
across a wide blue page
Every time I see one,
I say Hi to Ed
somewhere out there.

Sky Dreams

A rainbow covers
my naked body.

Then I'm standing
on top of the moon.

The stars shine down on me,
ALL OF THEM MIRACLES.

"Reach up to touch us,"
they tell me,
"and we'll come down
to bless you!"

YES!

Published In <u>Dream Network Journal</u> 1995

Awareness at Fifty:
The Greatest Thing About Getting Older

On a plane to Boston
when I could still see
the cars on roads
and where they go,
I had an awareness
very important to me.

It came not at twenty
or thirty or even forty.
Having the perspective,
the distance,
the understanding
why I took certain roads
but avoided others.
Why I turned right
instead of left
or backed up.
How I dealt with accidents
or one way streets
or road construction
or even dead ends.

It was only at fifty
I could really see
the big picture
laid out in front of me.

All Alone
(Written at age 15)

I'm all alone and feeling so blue,
All alone and wanting you.
All alone with your memory so dear,
All alone with a tear so near,
All alone seeing before me your tender eyes.
All alone hearing once more your wistful sighs,
All alone seeming to hold your faithful hand
All alone seeming to walk somewhere in a forbidden land,
All alone there too yet unwilling to return.
All alone here and having so much to learn,
All alone and praying for your love.
All alone forgetting still that you're up above
All alone with oh so many endless lonesome days,
All alone with a terrible ache that stays,
Yes, all alone with my dreams,
All alone and exiled it seems.

And the Lake Flows On

Ed dead a year and a week ago.

He's at peace.
He's at peace.
He's at peace.
And he would want us
to be at peace.

Words that come to me as my sons and I
came home from the hospital
after saying our final goodbyes
to my husband and their father.

And the lake flows on.

A year of change.
Of being on my own.
Taking care of everything:
house, cars, food
repairs, insurance, bills.
Learning many new things
in the daily process.

And the lake flows on.

Going back on the Singles' Scene.
Meeting many new friends.
Especially several special men.

And the lake flows on.

Evolving into my new self
even more outgoing than in the past.
Out on a limb and waiting passionately,
my Mantra from years ago still so today

though T.S. Eliot's line more significant now,
"I'm here, there or elsewhere. In my Beginning."

And the lake flows on.

I dance and dance and dance
whenever I get the chance
Contra. Blues. Waltz. Polka.
Swing, Square. Rock and Roll.
Slow. Fast. Or in between.

I talk a lot to people
about the world, about my books.
Handing out business cards,
flyers, bookmarks about them and me.
Most of all it seems, I wait
for friends to call, to visit, to email.

And the lake flows on.

I've reached the end of the four seasons
"Mother Nancy" told me
I had to get through
after Ed's death.
I've cried a well.
Laughed a bushel.
Danced a barrel of fun.
Swam an ocean.
Talked a canyon.

And the lake flows on.

Where do I go from here?
I can't imagine getting married again
though in some reality
two of my current friends
of the male persuasion
some kind of possibilities.

And the lake flows on.

More books to publish.
More writing to revise.
Whatever stories and poems
and plays and novels
waiting in the wings
of my imagination to be born.

And the lake flows on.

Where will the rest of my Life take me?
Where will it lead me?
Where will it send me?
Further out of myself?
Further into other endeavors?
Further into an exciting unknown
beyond here and now?

And the lake flows on and on and on....

Ah, Joy!

Some time after
her husband died,
a woman of a certain age
announced to family and friends,

"Now I'm going
to get back
to some degree
of normalcy."

How could she have realized then
that she was opening herself
like a flower from bud to blossom
to a New Life?
New Beginning?
New Love?

Never knowing
who or what awaits us
around the next corner
of the streets of our lives,
we walk or run
and sometimes stumble

holding on for dear life
to the Hope that a New Joy
will one day envelope us
like the inviting arms
of a lover.

Dear Elizabeth Hannah

We're all anxiously awaiting
your Coming Out Day!

Especially your Mom
and of course your dear Dad, my son.

Not to mention me,
your Grandma-to-be for the first time.

And your Granddad-in-spirit waiting on the Other Side
who's looked forward to you for years.

And then your two fine uncles-to-be
such "Lovas" in their own rights.

Oh, Liz or Beth or Izzy,
whatever you'll be called,

I sense your Granddad had a lot to do
with your being on the way

much more than the genetics
you'll learn about one day.

Oh, little Honey Darling,
all these months you've been kicking away

inside your Mom
practicing your Grand Entrance.

While your Dad put together your stroller,
a gift from your other Grandma.

And soon he'll do the same
for your white crib from me.

May you grow up to be
a strong and confident,

loving and kind woman
gloriously alive in your own special skin

open to the wondrous world
awaiting you with numerous possibilities.

May you live and thrive and dance and sing
in this beautiful outside place you're about to enter.

Yes, on some unconscious level
you'll miss the sanctuary of your Mom's womb

But out here with all of us
you'll have so much more

to learn and grow from
and most of all to become.

Get all the beauty rest you can
in these last few weeks, Elizabeth Hannah.

You're about to make your Fine Debut
onto this World's Stage very soon.

With much love,
Grandma Rose

And The Flow Continues

"Man, he lives in jerks - baby born an' a man dies, an' that's a jerk
- gets a farm an' loses his farm, an' that's a jerk. Woman, it's all
one flow, like a stream, little eddies, little waterfalls, but the
river, it goes right on. Woman looks at it like that."
Ma Joad from <u>The Grapes of Wrath</u> by John Steinbeck

Floooooooooooooooooooooooooooooooooooowing movement
streams surging-gurgling-whooshing

Going with the flow
Told years ago
that I had Buddhist tendencies

The Flow
The Stream
The Water
The Ocean
The Power
The Calm
The In
The Out

What does Flowing really mean?

Going with the punches.
Accepting challenges
with grace, calm, serenity.
And even joy.

What does flowing really mean?

Hanging loose.
Being ready for whatever.
The constant whatever.
The disturbing whatever.

The disgusting whatever.
The discouraging whatever.
The wondrous whatever.
The weird whatever.
The wild whatever.

What does flowing really mean?

Staying on an even keel
of up and down,
of in and out.
Tide controlled.
Moon controlled .

Flowing Flying Freeing
As my friend Don put it,
"Flying is great
if you're grounded."

How flow and fly free
and stay grounded
at the same time?

How be up, over and beyond
and yet in touch with the earth?

What does that mean?
Ground-ed
Earth-ed
Down to earth
To the ground
Feet on solid ground

Flying but staying on ground:
Key oxymoron of life.
Flying yet Grounded.

How flow yet be still?
How be tide in and tide out
yet stand on shore earthbound?

How stand loose and free
yet in touch with the earth?

Flow out of water.
Flow on ground.
Be flow.
Be ground.
Be stream.
Be earth.

What does all this mean
for me in class,
at home,
inside myself?

It's essentially
the same stance wherever.
Keep a cool flow.
Stand connected to the earth.
Flow with the surges of the tides
and the hardness of the earth.

Being is flowing.
Flowing is being.
Flying yet grounded
in glory and grace

How fly free
and flow at once
at the same time?

It's all a state
of mind and body.

Holistic being.
Full being.
Totality of one.
One with the land.
One with the water.
Flowing in and out.
Being flow.

And so the flow continues...

Menstrual flowing.
Menopausal flowing without flowing.
Flowing with the sap of life inside and out.
Flowing the answer to stress, heart attack and strokes.
Flowing what it means to be woman.
Calm and giving and understanding of herself
first and foremost and deepest.
Then flowing with others in her life mission.

Rose's stories, poems and essays have appeared in the following publications, among others:

Association for the Study of Dreams Newsletter
Burning Light
Dream Network Journal
Futuremics
Ginseng
Ideas Plus of The English Journal
Jungian Literary Criticism
Mad Alley
Networker of the Women Business Owners
  of Montgomery County, Maryland
New Women - New Church
Pablo Lennis
Pittsburgh Mercy
The Critic
The Dana California Literary Society
The Journal of the National Association of Poetry Therapy
The Journal of the National Council of Teachers of English
The Maryland English Journal
The Merton Seasonal

Lifetime Television Welcomed Author Rose Gordy to Hit TV Show The Balancing Act

On June 24th 2011 Lifetime TV interviewed Rose Gordy about her dramatic life and her book "Unsettled Lives"

PRLog (Press Release) (Pompano Beach, FL) After the economy crashed in 2008, many people lost their homes and nest eggs, but worst of all they were left with unsettled lives and uncertainty. With the economic crisis ongoing, people are searching for solace, resolution and a new acceptable normal. On June 24th, 2011, The Balancing Act TV show on Lifetime interviewed Rose Gordy about how she has weathered the storm and her new book "Unsettled Lives."

Author and dream counselor Rose Gordy spent thirteen years of her early life as a nun effectively cut off from the "the world of the flesh and the devil." Through her experiences in the convent as well as decades of teaching in the classroom, she has woven a compelling story honoring the lives lost and changed forever by triumph and adversity.

"Unsettled Lives - A Collection of Short Stories" presents numerous tales of people caught in the second-guessing, soul-searching, and uncertain decision-making periods of their lives. In dealing with their lives of quiet and not so quiet desperation, the book's characters may rise above the pain and face new tomorrows with hope and joy. Or perhaps some of them may find their fate in hapless distress and melancholy. What threads of life's twists and turns will determine the direction and destiny that awaits them?

"Having Rose Gordy on 'The Balancing Act' has brought yet another inspiring story of perseverance to women, one that will have a real impact, and help them balance their lives. This is the essence of solutions-based programming, and we're proud that we can bring this to a wide audience."

To view the interview, please visit www.Rosewords.com.

"Into the Green Unknown" and Other Science Fiction Stories - Now Available in Paperback

Attention Earth People... Special Announcement about an Interstellar Book by Rose of Maryland

PRLog (Press Release) – Heralding the release of Rose Gordy's book, "Into the Green Unknown," a collection of 21 science fiction stories and 6 poems, available now at Rosewords.com.

Years in the making, these astounding adventures range from everyday events turned bizarre, to fantastic realms under Earth's oceans, to incredible worlds beyond human perception. Stories such as "The Announcement," "Living Waters At Lucia," and "The Man From Somewhere Else" take readers to strange places they can't possibly journey. Or can they...?

In "Subterfuge," will Madame President be able to protect L.A. from take over by mind-controlling visitors? In "Lost Tides," can two nervous parents protect their children from a celestial disaster and its ramifications? In "The Genetic Casino," will the abducted Ronatta want to discover how she was chosen or remain ignorant and blissful? At the frenetic pace modern science is progressing these tales may be science fact by the time you cast an eye over them. That is, if they have not already transpired....

So join us for a jaunt on the Earth, in the Earth, in the Clouds, and among the Stars.

"Into the Green Unknown" is available now in paperback for only $14.99 and can be ordered at http://www.Rosewords.com. At Rosewords.com you can learn more about Rose Gordy's books and other projects. Bon Voyage!

ISBN: 1456528904

The Ladies Baltimore: Mothers and Daughters Alone and Together - A New Book

A riveting and sweeping account of several seemingly divergent women in Baltimore, MD.

PRLog (Press Release) – Author and dream counselor Rose Gordy spent thirteen years of her early life as a nun effectively cut off from the world. In spite of the conditions within the church, she managed to leave and make a life for herself including getting married and having three sons. Through her experiences in the convent as well as decades of teaching in the classroom, she has woven a compelling story honoring the lives lost and changed forever by adversity.

In "The Ladies Baltimore: Mothers and Daughters Alone and Together," an aged nun, a depressed waitress, and a lively teenage girl cross paths on a luncheon cruise in the Baltimore Harbor. Each woman will have a succession of unexpected and unique experiences related to mothers and daughters and to the various men in their lives. Spanning eight decades, the story organically unwinds in non-linear fashion as does life.

But will emotional resistance to the unknown lead them to destroy their vital links to the past? Or will they, through a cascading series of apparently chance encounters and fateful incidences around Baltimore, finally realize how they are profoundly connected? Perhaps time will tell if their lives are sublime results of synchronicity or merely chance encounters.

Also don't forget to visit the avant-garde Rosewords.com website, where you can find the latest on Rose Gordy's books and other projects. Thank you for your curiosity.

"The Ladies Baltimore" is available now in paperback for $14.99 and can be ordered through the publisher's website:
http://www.Rosewords.com   ISBN:978-0-557-418718

"Unsettled Lives" - A Collection of Short Stories - Available Now at Rosewords.com
A wide-ranging collection of short stories delving into the unstrung lives and rattled experiences of modern society.

PRLog (Press Release) – Rosewords Books is pleased to announce a new book by Rose Gordy and a completely redesigned Rosewords website. Rose's latest book is duly titled "Unsettled Lives - A Collection of Short Stories" and is now available for purchase on the state-of-the-art Rosewords Books website, http://www.Rosewords.com. This is the third book by Rose of Maryland, following "Into The Green Unknown" and "The Ladies Baltimore."

"Unsettled Lives - A Collection of Short Stories" presents numerous tales of people caught in the second-guessing, soul-searching, and uncertain decision-making periods of their lives. Will the myriad characters opt for the "right" path seemingly laid out for them? Yes, they may eventually find their way... but all too often they shall otherwise stumble into unexpected and unique journeys we call the "Human Experience."

Throughout 21 short stories, numerous situations of emotional and social consequence will be offered to the reader. In "Lila, The Love of His Lonely Life," will Charles ever come to grips with his ephemeral obsession? What is Sister Alberta in "Masquerades" aiming to discover by ingenious cloak-and-dagger operations? Furthermore, what could the doctor In "Joy's Esperanza" tell open-minded Joy that would send her into serious self-doubt?

So please join us for psychological jaunts into the various lives within "Unsettled Lives" ... and don't forget to choose the right door in your own.

"Unsettled Lives" is available in paperback for $14.99 and can be ordered through http://www.Rosewords.com.

ISBN: 1456420097

Author Rose Gordy's e-books are now available on Apple's iBookstore and Amazon's Kindle

Rosewords Books has released Rose's published tomes for the iPad, iPhone, and Kindle e-Readers

PRLog (Press Release) – Rosewords Books is pleased to announce the publication of Rose Gordy's four books in electronic book format. With e-book sales now surpassing print book sales on Amazon, the state of the book business is transitioning to a new and exciting era. Accordingly, Rosewords Books now has e-books for sale on Apple's iBookstore, where over 100 million e-books have been sold, and Amazon's Kindle Store, the industry leader in e-book sales.

Before the advent of electronic books, author and dream counselor Rose Gordy spent thirteen years of her early life as a nun effectively cut off from the world. In spite of the conditions within the church, she managed to leave and make a life for herself including getting married and having three sons. Through her experiences in the convent as well as decades of teaching in the classroom, she has written books which honor the lives lost and changed forever by triumph and adversity.

Her four books are titled "Stairs to the Attic," "Unsettled Lives," "The Ladies Baltimore: Mothers and Daughters Alone and Together" and "Into the Green Unknown." All are available at Rosewords.com.

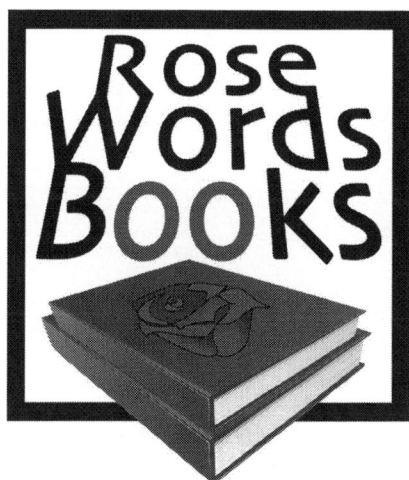

www.Rosewords.com

Made in the USA
Charleston, SC
07 August 2012